B·U·L·U

AFRICAN WONDER DOG

BY
DICK HOUSTON

Random House 🏠 New York

Visit us on the Web! www.randomhouse.com/kids

Educators and librarians, for a variety of teaching tools, visit us at www.randomhouse.com/teachers

Library of Congress Cataloging-in-Publication Data
Houston, Dick.
Bulu, African wonder dog / by Dick Houston. — 1st ed.
p.   cm.
ISBN 978-0-375-84723-3 (trade) — ISBN 978-0-375-94720-9 (lib. bdg.) —
ISBN 978-0-375-89307-0 (e-book)
1. Dogs—Zambia—Biography—Juvenile literature. 2. Wildlife conservation—Zambia—Juvenile
literature. I. Title.
SF426.2H675 2010
636.7092'9—dc22
2009015804

Cover photographs: Courtesy of Steve and Anna Tolan.
Interior photographs: Courtesy of Colleen Brink, pp. 210, 236; Dick Houston, p. 251;
Lari Shea, p. 268; Steve and Anna Tolan, pp. ii, 5, 18, 39, 49, 71, 73, 76, 87, 89, 98, 100, 111, 119,
128, 133, 137, 139, 142, 147, 149, 157, 159, 169, 187, 257, 307, 312, 318.

Map by Dick Houston

Printed in the United States of America

10 9 8 7 6 5 4 3 2 1

First Edition

Random House Children's Books supports the First Amendment and celebrates the right to read.

To Anna and Steve Tolan, champions of Zambia's
endangered wildlife and guardians of its wild orphans.

And to Saint Francis of Assisi, the patron saint
of animals, who was the first to give animals a voice,
and their dignity.

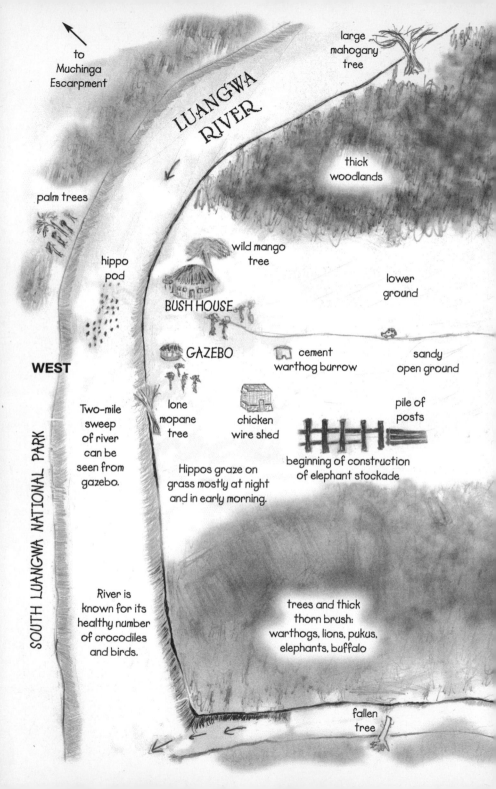

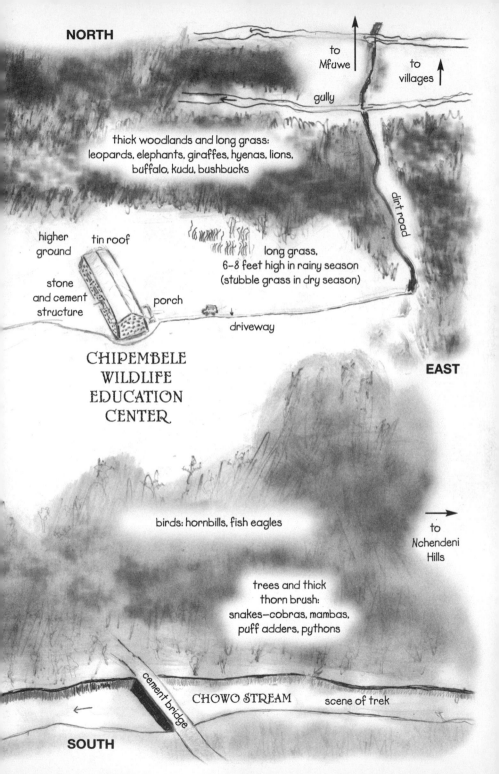

This is a true story. . . .

I first met Bulu several years ago in Zambia's Luangwa Valley. I was at the anti-poaching headquarters of the South Luangwa Conservation Society (SLCS). As president of Elefence International (an elephant conservation group), I was meeting with Rachel McRobb, the head of the SLCS, and its ranger force. While we were discussing plans to build the rangers an anti-poaching base, the two-way radio crackled to life. It was Anna Tolan of the Chipembele Wildlife Education Center, calling with an emergency from a nearby village. A hyena was caught in a snare. The animal was alive, but the wire had cut deep into its neck. She was using the radio of a Zambia Wildlife Authority (ZAWA) officer on the scene.

We drove to the scene and Rachel got out of the vehicle. Within minutes, she had calculated the drug dosage required, prepared the darting syringe, and loaded it into a carbon dioxide air rifle. Then she walked within several feet of the hyena, knelt down, aimed her rifle, and fired. *Pop.* The dart found its mark in the animal's left hip. Five minutes later, the hyena was out cold. Using large wire cutters, Rachel removed the snare.

The ZAWA officer gave us permission to move the hyena to Chipembele for treatment. An hour later, we drove up to the wildlife center. A man stepped off the porch of a long cement building to greet us. It was Anna's husband, Steve. We then carried the unconscious hyena into an open-air shed. It had a three-foot-high stone wall base, with chicken wire walls encircling support poles. We set the hapless animal on the floor. Rachel examined the hyena's neck and saw that the injury was not life-threatening. She cleaned the wound and injected antibiotics. After its full recovery, the hyena would be released back into the wild.

As I turned to leave the shed, I saw something peering through the chicken wire. It was a white dog with brown markings and a pointy face. It was standing on tiptoe against the stone wall, watching the hyena. Then the dog cocked its head to study me. "That's Bulu." Steve chuckled, noticing my surprise. "Let me introduce you."

And from that moment on, I was in love with Bulu. As Steve and Anna and I became close friends, I learned of his incredible story. Over the years, I've been privileged to see him in action in the bush. As you will read in these pages, Bulu is one of the most extraordinary dogs who ever lived.

—Dick Houston
May 2010

"**D**on't get a dog if you're going to live in the African bush," Mitch warned Steve and Anna as they sat in the shade of their gazebo overlooking the Luangwa River. "Several years ago, some friends of mine lost a dog to a leopard. Snatched him right off the porch." Mitch looked to the river, where a crocodile was crawling onto a sandbar. "I've run safaris for nearly forty years in the Luangwa Valley. I've never seen a pet survive here beyond a few months." He gestured at the hippo pod midriver, grumbling in the steam-bath heat. "Need I remind you?" He grinned his crooked smile. "There's tons of risks for a dog in the Zambian bush."

"Anna and I know a few things about risks," Steve said with a wink at Anna as she poured tea into tin cups. The two smiled as they glanced over at their African-style house, fifty yards from the gazebo. It was a one-room circular *rondavel*, made of wood and straw with a thatched roof. It rested like a huge dried-up cupcake under a wild mango tree. Inside, a kerosene refrigerator sweated to keep perishable food cold, an old propane stove smoked their meals, and a shower rained river water behind a wicker screen. Cobras slithered inside when they forgot to close the door. Scorpions dropped onto the mosquito net over their bed. Lions' roars rattled the reed walls. But despite the risks, Steve and Anna loved life in Zambia's untamed South Luangwa Valley. They were living their dream.

"Nevertheless," Mitch continued, "this is no place for a dog."

"Oh now, Mitch," Anna persisted. "Didn't you just say that there were puppies for sale at the old crocodile farm?"

"You really *are* determined, aren't you?" Mitch shook his head and brushed back his long white hair.

"When Anna makes up her mind, there's no turning back." Steve laughed. "Why else do you think we left England to live here?"

"Okay, if you must know. Yesterday I saw Hank at the croc farm. There were five pups in the litter. Four are sold, but nobody wants the last one. His father was a Jack Russell. Terriers are usually full of energy and bouncing off the walls. But this one is unresponsive. Too quiet. Its legs are too long and it has a pointy face. You should look around for a different dog."

Anna thought for a moment. "Why should we look further?" She sat back in her canvas chair, folded her arms, and narrowed her eyes at Mitch. "Sounds to me like this dog *is* different."

"Well, I guess in a way he is." Mitch shrugged. "Look, if you get the dog, you must know this. Owning one will bring you nothing but heartache. Sooner or later he *will* get bitten by a tsetse fly and be infected with the trypanosome parasite. It causes sleeping sickness. Most wild animals are immune. But the disease is the number one killer of domestic animals in Africa." He reached for the teapot. "And keep your eye on him. After all, he's part terrier. If he goes chasing after something in the bush . . . he may get *eaten*."

Like a drunken rhino, the Land Rover swayed between holes and ruts on the muddy road. It was November, the beginning of the rainy season. Steve and Anna turned onto a narrow track lined with a carpet of sprouting grass. A faded CROCODILE FARM sign peeked through the green brush. The old cement pools and tanks that once held crocodiles were now cracked with weeds and roots. The creatures had been raised there for their skins until the business, like the crocs, went belly up. The grounds were now being converted into lodging facilities for tourists. African workers on ladders were thatching new roofs for the cottages.

Steve parked the Land Rover beside a single-story house with a red tin roof. Hank, a stocky man in baggy shorts, stepped off the porch to greet them. "Sorry, my friends. We're fresh out of flat dogs!" he joked, *flat dogs* being the Zambian nickname for crocs.

Anna laughed as she and Steve climbed out of the truck. "We came to look at a *real* dog, actually."

"Only one left," said Hank. "A male. Come have a look."

Hank led them inside. He opened the door to a dimly lit room and pulled back a burlap curtain at the window. "Well, here he is." On the floor was an old cardboard box lined with a white blanket.

As their eyes adjusted to the light, a brown patch appeared on the blanket framing the head of a white puppy. The dog was curled up on his side, sleeping. The single brown spot on his back looked like it had dropped from a paintbrush. "He's so little," Anna said softly as she carefully picked him up and cradled him in her arms.

Steve looked at him closely. "There's something about his face. It's so familiar. I can't quite place it."

Anna glanced at Steve, who was now grinning at her. She smiled back. "Hank, I think we'll take him," she said. "How much do we owe you?"

"Dinner at your place—all I can eat. I'll get you a fresh box to take him home in."

"That won't be necessary." Anna cuddled the puppy close to her chest. "I brought Marty's bed."

"*Marty?*" said Hank.

"An old friend we had to leave behind in England," Anna answered in a thin voice.

"Oh, I see." Hank nodded, understanding. "A very *dear* old friend, I'm sure."

Steve steered the Land Rover toward home on the road that ran beside the river. Anna sat next to him holding the wicker dog bed on her lap. She put her hand on the puppy's warm little belly and remembered back fifteen years earlier. She and Steve were bringing Marty home—in the same wicker bed—to their cottage in Oxford. Marty was a border collie puppy, smart, alert, and affectionate from the start. For the next fifteen years, he went everywhere with Anna and Steve. Last year, however, just before leaving England to set up their new home in Zambia, they had to make an agonizing decision. Marty was far too old to survive the journey. They had to leave him behind in the care of Anna's elderly parents.

Now Anna was having second thoughts about getting *this* puppy. Was she really putting him in harm's way? Baboon troops were always hanging around the riverbank near the house. The males with their six-inchlong incisors were known to chase and kill baby impalas. Mother warthogs with dagger-like tusks slashed viciously at hyenas that ventured too close to their babies. At night, hippos surfaced silently like Navy SEALs to feed on the riverbank. How could she possibly expect a puppy to survive in the bush? Was she thinking *only* of herself in getting a dog?

A hard jolt in the road interrupted her worrying. The Land Rover lurched forward. The puppy remained asleep.

"I can't believe that didn't wake him," Steve said.

Anna looked down into the bed. "You don't suppose they were right about him, do you?"

"Right about what?"

"That he's *different*. That maybe he doesn't have much personality?"

Steve reached over and put his hand on the puppy's head. "You know, there's a world of difference between personality and character. My mother always told me that still waters run deep."

Anna smiled and thought how typical it was of Steve to see things other people missed. She looked at him as he concentrated on the road. He hadn't changed much since she met him seventeen years ago. His close-cropped hair was graying fast, but he still had his easy smile and boyish sense of humor. She shuddered when she thought how close she had come to losing him.

As the Land Rover rumbled along the road, she reflected on their first encounter. They were employed as police officers in Slough, England, working the same shift. Getting to know each other, they discovered a mutual passion for animals and hiking in the countryside. Anna had a degree in environmental science and had longed to work on wildlife conservation projects. But she could never find a position in her field. She confessed to Steve a wish she had had since she was a girl. A dream to go to Africa and see wild animals. Steve agreed that Africa would be the greatest adventure of all. They talked of traveling there together someday.

Then upsetting news. Steve was transferred from Slough to the Thames Valley Police Department in Oxford. When he left, Anna thought she would never see him again. But months later, Steve returned to Slough to give evidence in court. When the two saw each other at the police station, they realized how much they missed each other. Within two weeks, they were engaged. Months later, they married and set up home in Oxford. Soon afterward, Anna was hired to do undercover work tracking down stolen furniture, jewelry, and paintings. Her new detective job helped the couple save for their African dream. They planned to take off every year to explore the vast continent on their monthlong vacations.

Anna held tightly to the puppy's bed as Steve accelerated to forge through a three-foot gully, splashing water over the radiator. Here, the road threaded through a dense wood of mopane trees, their butterfly-shaped leaves fluttering in the breeze. Anna knew every feature of the secluded road that paralleled the Luangwa River, with the national park on the opposite bank. Wild animals ignored park boundaries and moved freely back and forth across the water. Anna and Steve loved the primitiveness of the river, just about the only one in all of Africa untouched by dams.

She remembered the first time they had driven on this road. It was on one of their many explorations of Africa. They had been to the Congo, Ghana, Senegal, Kenya, Tanzania, Namibia, Botswana, and many other African countries. Then one year they made a fateful decision. They were going to explore Zambia. From Lusaka, Zambia's capital city, they drove eastward over a rough track to South Luangwa National Park. Few tourists ever visited there because of its remoteness and terrible roads. It was love at first sight when they reached the edge of the cliffs at Muchinga Escarpment—the western wall of the Luangwa Valley. They gazed downward two thousand feet. An emerald ocean of treetops spread across an endless wilderness— hundreds and hundreds of square miles of woodlands, lagoons, and open grassland plains. Thirty-five miles in the distance, a river snaked its way through this hidden Eden. Reaching the valley floor, Steve and Anna were stunned. No other corner of Africa they'd been to had so many different species of animals in one location. There were buffalo by the thousands, giraffes, zebras, kudu, sables, eland, waterbuck, cheetahs, and more leopards per square mile than in any other place in Africa. There were over four hundred species of birds. The Luangwa River had the greatest concentrations of hippos and crocs on the continent. The valley had boasted a population of eight thousand rhinos and had been made famous for its awesome number of elephants, over a hundred thousand strong. The locals had fittingly named Luangwa the Valley of the Elephants.

The place had cast its spell. Anna remembered their last night of vacation before returning to England. They were camping on the riverbank under a dome of stars when they heard faint grunts in the distance. A goosebump sound more felt than heard. A calling. *Aaaaar . . . uummmmf . . . aaaaar . . . uummmmf.* She recalled every detail as though it were a scene from a favorite movie. It was the turning point in their lives.

"Listen," Steve had said. "Lions!" *Aaaaar . . . uummmmf . . . aaaaar . . . uummmmf.* He stood up in front of the campfire, his eyes shining with excitement. "We've got to live here, Anna." He turned to look at her as she sat in her canvas chair, sipping coffee. "How can we ever return to our old life in Oxford?"

Anna knew Steve loved their safaris, but she was surprised he wanted to live in Africa. "Steve," she said. "Be practical. We have jobs, our home—"

"Practical is for bankers," he interrupted. "I'll build a house here."

"But you've never built one before!"

"I'll learn."

"And pray tell, what will you make it out of? Straw and reeds?"

They laughed at themselves. His idea looked as frail as the house Steve planned to make.

"I guess it is a bit unrealistic." Steve looked up at the stars, from where the lions' voices seemed to have called. "Still . . . life is short. Everyone's forever planning for the future. No one lives in the moment anymore."

Like cold water, practicality doused the flare of Steve's spontaneity. Their police jobs awaited and bills had to be paid. Yet the ember of the dream still glowed. Long into the night they talked about the possibility of living in Luangwa after their retirement. But retirement seemed a million years away. Then one day after their return to England, fate stepped in.

Steve was on duty and got an emergency call. He raced to his squad car. While traveling at high speed, his car collided with another vehicle and ran straight into a wall. He was badly hurt, with serious back and neck damage. His injuries were severe enough that he could no longer work as a police officer. He was retired on medical disability.

Weeks after the shock of the accident, Anna remembered Steve's words. *Life is short. No one lives in the moment.* As Steve gradually healed, they decided that this was the time to live in the moment. Anna resigned her job at the police department, they sold their material possessions, and they made plans to live permanently in Zambia.

"Steve," Anna said. "Do you remember what people first thought when we told them we were leaving England to live in Africa?"

"Sure do! Most of them said it sounded *crazy.* The more polite ones said it sounded *different.*"

Anna reached into the bed and picked up the puppy. "Different, are you?" she whispered as she brought his face close to hers. "What shall we name you?" His eyes remained shut. She looked through the windshield and saw a fragment of the river flash between the trees.

The Land Rover turned onto the familiar track leading to their straw and grass house. When they came to a stop, Anna became uneasy. She could hear the grunting noise of the hippos. She remembered Mitch's warnings about getting a dog. *It will bring you nothing but heartache.*

"**H**ere's your new home, little guy," Steve said as he turned off the Land Rover's ignition. "Not a mansion— but the view's worth a million." Anna set the puppy back into the basket. Then she opened the door and stepped out to stretch her legs. She squinted at the setting sun glowing through the woods across the river. When she looked back into the truck, she was surprised. The puppy had climbed out of the basket and was standing on the seat, staring at her. His eyes, reflecting the sun's slanting rays, burned the color of amber.

"Will you look at that? He's studying you." Steve put his arms around Anna as he watched the puppy. "I can't help but think I've seen that face before."

"On an Egyptian tomb, maybe?" Anna marveled, studying the little face. "His eyes are lined like a pharaoh's."

Anna picked the puppy up off the seat and tried to hold him in her arms, but he squirmed and wanted down. She gently placed him on the ground. He turned his head into the breeze and drank in his first scent of the Luangwa. He then waddled unsteadily toward the river as Steve and Anna followed.

Screeeeeee screeeeeee screeeeeee. An eagle swooped low between the trees, talons clutching a fish. The puppy calmly looked up, his eyes following the eagle's sweeping path.

"Did you see that?" Steve said as he sat down on the sandy embankment. "The pup didn't flinch."

"That's what worries me. There are so many birds of prey here. Eagles, kites, hawks. One evening, I saw a martial eagle zero in on a mongoose near the river. Just like that, the eagle snatched him up and was *gone.*"

The puppy cocked his head toward the hippos clustered in the middle of the river. Their rumblings were carried by the wind. *Hummph hummph hummph.* Then his attention snapped to a skimmer bird gliding above the water's surface, its lower beak trawling for fish. The puppy was fascinated with everything he watched.

"I remember now," Steve said. "Months ago, downriver. I was trailing human tracks in the sand. Ivory poachers. Their prints superimposed on the tracks of an old bull elephant. The dimming light made it hard to see, and I had the feeling I was being watched. I looked to my left through the thornbushes and was startled by something staring at me. Intelligent eyes peering from a wide face. It was a wild dog. His round ears alert as radar. Behind him I could just make out the blur of his pack loping off. But he never moved. We just stared at each other. His eyes were dark amber." Steve turned his attention back to the puppy and then to Anna. "You know, in the local Nyanja language the word for wild dog is *bulu*."

Steve unlatched the creaky door of the house. The dark interior smelled like damp hay from the rains. He struck a match and lit one of the gas lanterns, pumping it to life. Honey-colored light slowly revealed a circular room crammed with primitive furnishings. Beside the old stove, four handmade chairs surrounded a table holding tin plates, pots, and pans. A blue African print cloth covered the mattress of a double bed beside a window facing the river. Shelves on a lopsided bookcase sagged with volumes on natural history, exploration, and paleontology. Against another wall, a pantry was jampacked with cans of milk, corned beef, beans, butter, oil, marmalade, and battered tin containers of flour, coffee, biscuits, tea, and sugar. A worn leather couch, sunken in the middle, sat beside the big ceramic watercooler. A leaky showerhead peeked above the bathroom's wicker partition. A Winchester Magnum rifle rested on a wall rack, and two dented steel ammunition cases were stacked beneath it. Cameras and binoculars hung from pegs beside the door. Red-print curtains added a splash of color to the brown straw walls. The high arched roof, like the inside of a wizard's hat, allowed heat to rise and kept the room cool.

Anna stood outside and looked up at the wild mango tree beside the house. Yellow fruit by the hundreds hung against the darkening sky. *Plop plop.* Some fruits dropped onto the roof. The puppy looked up, transfixed as they rolled onto the ground. Anna held his little face next to her cheek. "The elephants will be here soon, Bulu." She bent down and picked up a mango. "This is their favorite snack."

Anna stepped inside. Steve was opening a tin can at the kitchen table. "Fast-food tonight," he said. "Beans on buttered bread."

Anna set Bulu down on the cool cement floor. He immediately toddled over to investigate one of Steve's sandals. She stepped out to retrieve the dog bed from the Land Rover. When she returned, she found Bulu fast asleep, half inside the sandal.

"Chief Kakumbi will be here in two days," Steve said, plastering butter on his bread. "I'm a bit anxious. Let's hope he rents us the land. Our future here depends on his decision."

"We'd better serve him something besides beans, then," Anna said, sitting down at the table.

"Yes, beans have no dignity." Steve grinned. "Let's have a *braai*. We'll need a new propane can for the grill. I'll head off straightaway in the morning to get one. See if I can buy some fresh bream. Tastiest fish in the world. Then to the market for fresh fruit and vegetables."

"Everything must be festive." Anna turned her

attention to the shelves that held neatly folded stacks of clothes and sheets. "I can use the purple tie-dyed table-cloth. Wonder if we have enough—"

"—sweets!" Steve interrupted as he dropped a glob of beans on bread.

"Yes, we must have sweets." She looked over at Bulu crashed out on the sandal. "Let me think what I can make."

Anna got up from the table. Bulu didn't stir as she placed him and the shoe in the dog bed. "I think you may also need a new pair of sandals."

Vanilla-sweet mopane smoke filled the morning air and stirred Anna from her sleep. "Up and at 'em!" Steve said, bringing her tea. His hair was still damp from the shower. "I've fired up the old barrel. Should be enough hot water left for you." He grabbed his jacket and keys. "Back by late afternoon." He hurried out the door, forgetting to latch it behind him.

Anna pulled back the mosquito net and got up. Bulu was still slumbering with his sandal. She knelt down by the dog bed and kissed him on his little nose. He opened his eyes. "Time for your breakfast." At the kitchen table, Anna whipped together a mixture of egg yolks and milk. Just as she set the bowl on the floor, Bulu got to his feet. He eagerly lapped up all his food. She laughed as he instantly lay back down on his sandal and closed his eyes.

Anna then headed for the shower. She adjusted the hot water with cool water from the outside barrels and grabbed the shampoo and soap. The patter of water hitting the floor muffled the scream of an eagle somewhere close. Moments later, she turned off the spigot, toweled down, slipped into her khaki shirt and shorts, and stepped back into the room. Bulu was nowhere to be seen. She looked under the bed. Not there. "Bulu? Where are you?" Her eyes quickly scanned the room. Then she saw the door ajar. She thought of the screaming eagle and raced outside. *"Bulu? Bulu?"* she called, looking right and left. Nothing. She tried to keep from panicking as she searched the sandy, damp earth. Where were his prints? Then she found them, barely visible, among the crisscross of baboon, antelope, and genet cat tracks. They led from the house toward the river— where he would be exposed to the open sky!

Anna paced quickly, trying not to lose sight of the tracks. She emerged from the thickets onto the open embankment. And there was Bulu. Perfectly still, sitting on the bank. His head was cocked sideways as he watched a troop of baboons forty yards off at the water's edge. The troop was knuckle-walking along the riverbed, babies hitchhiking on their mothers' backs. Big, muscular males brought up the rear with macho attitude.

When the males spotted Anna, they started barking. Like a band of thieves caught in a raid, the baboons screamed and scrambled down the beach.

Anna scooped up the tiny puppy and held him tight. "Bulu," she choked. "Oh, Bulu. You must *never* again wander alone in the bush."

Wot *wot wot wot wot*. Something startled a pair of red-billed hornbills in the mango tree. Anna looked up from preparing for the evening's *braai,* setting dishes on the table in the gazebo. From where she stood, she could see only the top of the tree. Bulu, lying in a canvas chair at the table, raised his head and sniffed the air. He got to his feet and uttered a low growl, then a little bark.

"Why, Bulu, I've never heard you make a sound before! You *can* talk." Anna laughed. "That's only a couple of hornbills." *WOT WOT WOT WOT WOT.* Their alarm calls got louder as they flapped into the higher branches. "What in the world's bothering them? Let's go have a look."

Anna picked up Bulu and headed for the house. Suddenly the hornbills shot from the tree and the branches began to shake as though in an earthquake. A cascade of fruit showered down on the roof just as Anna stepped behind the house. Her heart stopped. Only ten yards away stood the rear end of an elephant! Rays of light etched every crease in his baggy hide, his sway belly, and his legs like dark chocolate, wet from crossing the river. The bull's massive head was thrust into the tree, his trunk coiled like a python around one of the upper branches. He had not caught Anna's scent since she was downwind.

Anna held Bulu tightly, feeling his little heart beating rapidly. She started silently backing up. The elephant shook the branches even harder. The tree became like a giant piñata showering the ground with mangoes. Anna continued backward around the house until out of sight, then paced quickly toward the gazebo. She dropped into her chair as adrenaline left her knees weak. Bulu glared back at the tree and growled.

Twilight dimmed the landscape. Anna walked from the house carrying a large wicker basket of food in one arm and Bulu in the other. Reaching the gazebo, she set Bulu on a chair and the basket on the table. In the distance, she could hear the rumble of the Land Rover bringing Chief Kakumbi. She was anxious. Would the chief rent them the land to build a wildlife center? If not, would she and Steve have to leave the valley?

Anna looked around the gazebo, fussing over the table setting. She lit candles on the table and the lanterns hanging from the roof. Then she stepped outside to check the *braai* and the driftwood for the bonfire. The sky was clearing. Fortunately, an afternoon shower had ended. She set up three safari chairs. Steve had chosen the riverbank as the ideal setting to make their pitch to the chief. Beside the woodpile, a canvas tarp was tied down over a waist-high mound. Later in the night, they would unveil what lay beneath.

As she lit the grill, the Land Rover came up the driveway. Chief Kakumbi was seated beside Steve. Anna smoothed her blue caftan and straightened her posture. Steve stopped the truck, got out, and opened the door for the chief. Dressed smartly in a green cotton shirt and pressed white slacks, Chief Kakumbi had a noble presence. Fluent in English and well educated, the chief was an articulate man of wise counsel. Anna stepped forward, put her hands together, and did a little curtsy, the traditional Zambian greeting of respect. "Chief Kakumbi. Steve and I welcome you with happy hearts. Thank you for coming to listen to our proposal."

Chief Kakumbi bowed slightly. "I'm looking forward to it."

Anna and Steve escorted the chief into the gazebo

and gestured for him to take his seat. But Chief Kakumbi suddenly hesitated and looked down at his chair of honor. Bulu was sitting in it, staring up at the chief! "Oh, I'm so sorry!" Anna apologized, remembering that a dog near a dining table is an insult in certain African cultures. Chief Kakumbi continued to gaze at Bulu a moment, as though studying him. Then he fixed his penetrating eyes on Anna and Steve. "Very unusual. I have not seen a dog like this before. He does not cower like the dogs in the villages. His eyes show spirit."

"He *has* spirit," Anna said, greatly relieved the chief was not offended. "He's already wandered off on his own. His name is Bulu." She quickly leaned over to pick him up. "I'll take him back to the house."

"That won't be necessary." Chief Kakumbi placed his hand on the puppy's head. "A *bulu* is independent."

Anna then set Bulu on a different chair near the table. She smiled at Steve, knowing that Bulu had charmed the chief.

Bream fillets sizzled on the *braai* as smoke streamed into the dusky sky. When Steve started to fork the fish off the grill, he felt a presence. Something was nearby. A large shadow was moving between the trees just beyond the house. He peered into the darkness, but the shadow was gone. He put the fish onto a platter and headed back to the gazebo, now aglow in golden light. "I think we have an uninvited guest," he said. "A very big one."

"Probably the same elephant I saw earlier," Anna said as she filled the wineglasses. The table was laden with fresh bread, sweet potatoes, tomatoes, bananas, cheese, and a caramel custard pudding.

"I remember a *chipembele* . . . a rhino," Chief Kakumbi said. "He crashed through a wedding feast in our village. Everyone ran for cover. He knocked over the big beer pot on the way out. A *very* unhappy village."

Steve thought a moment as he took a sip of wine. "That was our only disappointment when we first came here. Not seeing any rhinos. The tour books boasted that Luangwa had Africa's biggest concentration, but we never saw even *one*. How could they *all* vanish within two decades?"

"Because of some corrupt, evil politicians," Chief Kakumbi answered. "Their greed fueled the black-market trade. They smuggled rhino horns to Asia to be ground up for folk medicine. To Yemen to be made into handles for daggers. Poachers did the politicians' dirty work, slaughtering the rhinos with machine guns. Because each horn could sell for thirty thousand dollars, you can see why—"

"—the rhino's now extinct in Zambia," Steve said angrily, stabbing a potato onto his plate with a knife. "We wondered why the elephants weren't extinct here too. The only ones we saw hung around the lodges and ranger posts."

"That's because they sought *protection*," Chief Kakumbi explained. "The valley had become a killing field in the 1970s and 1980s. Poachers used machine guns to mow down entire herds. All for ivory. Smuggled to China and Japan to be carved into souvenirs. Over ninety thousand elephants in the valley slaughtered." He put down his wineglass and gazed into the distance. "The pressure on elephants is not just from poachers. Each year, more people are moving here from outside the valley—farming on and closer to the park's boundaries. Consequently, elephants compete with farmers over the same food and water. These conflicts often turn deadly—for both people and elephants."

"Do the farmers resent the park?" Anna asked.

"Most of them," the chief said. "They want *that* land too. They see no purpose for conserving elephants and other wildlife. Many people here have become greedy—wasting the valley's natural resources. They chop down the trees for charcoal businesses, causing erosion. They *never* replant. They overfish the river. They trap wild animals for—"

Ruff ruff ruff ruff ruff. Bulu jumped down from the chair and, barking frantically, waddled his little legs toward the edge of the gazebo. Then he stopped, stood still, and looked *up.* Steve raised his hand for silence. Anna picked up Bulu and tiptoed around to snuff the lanterns and candles. The gazebo was plunged into darkness. A musky odor filled the air. Only twenty feet away, darkly outlined against the stars, was the bull elephant. The faint light revealed only a glint of his great tusks.

Steve, Anna, and the chief sat silently at the table. Bulu, in Anna's lap, was spellbound and quiet. The bull slowly took a few steps toward the gazebo. Unable to see below the roof, he snaked his trunk out toward the edge of the thatch and caught the detested human scent. *WHOOOSH.* The bull expelled air through his trunk. Then, seemingly contemptuous of the nearby people, he raised his head high and slowly turned around. With kingly bearing, he walked down the steep riverbank and was gone.

A shower of bonfire sparks popped and flew. Steve removed the charred coffeepot from the fire and brought it over to the chief and Anna, seated in the safari chairs on the riverbank. Bulu was at their feet.

Ooooooh woooooooOOP ooooooohh woooooooOOP. Bulu turned his head toward the distant call. "Moon dogs, Bulu," Steve said, pouring coffee into tin cups. "Hyenas. Don't mess with 'em. They can bite holes in coffeepots."

Steve returned to his chair, purposely placed next to the canvas-covered mound. "I saw a dead hyena in a snare last week," he said. "The wire worked like a noose around his neck, nearly decapitating him."

"It's the horrible bush meat business," Chief Kakumbi said. "It's yet another crooked trade making politicians richer." He shook his head in disgust. "In some African countries there's very little control."

"You mean there's *no* control!" Anna stressed. "West Africa is the worst. They've logged over ninety percent of their forests into wastelands. *Ate* most of their antelope, monkeys, elephants, giraffes, chimpanzees—even the birds! About all that's left in the meat markets are *rodents.*"

"Luangwa could fast become another West Africa," Steve said as he stood up, starting to make his pitch. "I have something to show you, Chief Kakumbi." He grabbed his knife and walked over to the mound. Slashing the twine on each corner of the canvas, he pulled back the tarp. The chief sat upright in his chair. Gleaming in the firelight were hundreds of wire snares, heaped four feet high, coiled like cobras. "Smuggled from Lusaka," Steve continued. "They were found hidden in one of the village granary bins in our own backyard. This stockpile is only the beginning."

"Chief Kakumbi," said Anna. "The local people don't need to poach wild animals for food. There's plenty of fish in the river. Most of the smoked bush meat is smuggled to city markets or exported overseas to African expatriates. People defend eating bush meat by saying it is an African tradition." She purposely made a point of gesturing at the snares. "*Greed* should never be a tradition."

The chief sat back in his chair, then fixed his piercing stare on Steve and Anna. "But what can you—only two people—do about it? If you challenge these old traditions, you will make enemies of the elders. They will not listen. You cannot change them."

"We do not plan to change the elders," Steve said.

"But we think we know who will listen. The *children*." He paused a moment to let the idea sink in.

Anna got up to stand beside Steve. "The real enemy of wildlife is ignorance. The elders do not see that the old path leads to the end of their natural resources. Let the children be the eyes for the future of Luangwa. A wildlife education can teach them to replant trees. Fish responsibly. Fertilize the soil. Conserve wild animals to protect the food chain."

"Anna and I will pay for the construction of a wildlife education center here with our own savings," Steve offered. "Chief Kakumbi. All we ask is that you rent to us more of your land."

The chief sat silently staring. Then he stood up and looked slowly around before speaking. "My people have owned this land along the river for as long as I can remember. I love it." He walked over to the embankment, then bent over and picked up a handful of earth. He let it sift through his fingers. "I have reached my final decision. I can no longer rent you this land."

Anna and Steve looked at each other, stricken. How had they failed?

"But I will"—Chief Kakumbi turned to face them—"*give* you this piece of land. For the wildlife center *and* for your home."

Anna put her hands to her face, fighting back tears. Steve was speechless. He put his arm around Anna as she leaned into his shoulder.

"You have the heart for this place," Chief Kakumbi said as he stood tall in the firelight. "You shall build this wildlife center. You shall have the ears of our children."

Anna had to think a moment before responding to the chief, still stunned by his offer. She gathered her composure, then spoke softly. "Thank you, thank you for allowing Steve and me to be a voice for Luangwa." She gazed down at the pile of snares. "We have much work ahead of us." Anna walked over to the embankment and picked up Bulu. "I think we need to teach the worth of animals as *individuals*. That they have spirit. We need to reach the children's *hearts*. But how?"

For the first time that evening, there was a glint of a smile in Chief Kakumbi's eyes. He reached over and touched the little white dog. "Perhaps Bulu will show them the way?"

The dry season had crept into the valley. Month after month, scorching winds nearly suffocated all life from Luangwa. Temperatures soared over a hundred degrees Fahrenheit. Wild animals were gathered in great numbers around shrinking water holes. Grasses were reduced to stubble. The apple-green leaves of the woodlands had shriveled to dark reds and browns. The hippos had vanished from the shrunken pools in front of the house and moved to the deep lagoons a few miles away. Only their prints were left in the dried mud. The blistering white-hot sun had stolen the river. It was now October, the last month of winter—the hottest and driest time in the valley.

First light of dawn snuffed out the stars as the door of the bush house opened. Steve, shirtless in the oppressive heat, walked out holding a roll of blueprints. Bulu appeared at the doorway and trotted behind him. Steve stopped, yawned, and stretched. Bulu stopped, yawned, and stretched. "Your legs are getting longer and longer, Bulu. Like a Jack Russell on stilts." Steve laughed. *Ruff ruff ruff.* "Your voice is getting deeper too. Like a teenager's." He reached down to scratch Bulu behind the ears. "Not bad for a one-year-old."

The two headed toward the construction site, on a rise a thousand feet from the river—the location chosen for the future wildlife center. About a dozen men were unloading cinder blocks and stones from a transport truck. Others were pushing wheelbarrows of wet cement. Steve walked over to a steel worktable set beside a foundation of cinder blocks. At seventy-two by forty feet, it looked like the outline for an Olympic-sized pool. Once constructed, the wildlife center would have an ideal view of the river to the west and the Nchendeni Hills to the east.

"I'm off for my walk," Anna announced as she suddenly appeared beside the worktable. She had a knapsack on her back and a camera slung over her shoulder.

"Where to?" Steve asked as he unrolled the blueprints.

"A little ways downriver." Anna looked at Bulu standing near the foundation. "But you, Mister Bulu. You're staying *here*." She turned and headed toward the riverbed. "Don't forget to lock him in the house while I'm gone," she said over her shoulder, "or he'll follow me. I don't need Bulu spoiling any more of my pictures."

"Will do," Steve said, half listening as he studied the blueprints.

Anna walked to the embankment and heard something. *Too-hee-tee too-hee-tee.* It was the whistle call of the Klaas cuckoo. Her eyes scanned the trees. Then she spotted it high atop a naked branch. A tiny green bird with an ivory breast. *Too-hee-tee too-hee-tee.* Her heart soared every time she heard its song. She climbed down the bank and walked onto the drying riverbed.

Every day for the past several months, Anna would grab her camera and take off hiking, either north or south along the Luangwa. She'd been making a visual record of Luangwa's birdlife to display at the wildlife center. The dry season was the perfect time for photographing waterbirds feeding on fish in the shrinking river. Herons, yellow-billed storks, and pelicans would be a few of the species she could capture on film.

Bulu had increasingly become a problem on these walks. Up until he was about six months old, he stuck close to her, shy of animals. But by being exposed to the bush on daily jaunts, he'd become more confident. Then at nine months his legs seemed to lengthen overnight. He discovered that *long* legs took you places fast!

Waterbirds quickly became the target for chase games. Just as Anna would set up her tripod, Bulu would flush whatever bird she was trying to photograph. No species was exempt from the great chase. Guinea fowl, sandpipers, crested cranes, plover, ducks, quail, grouse, and geese. Even the sacred ibis wasn't sacred to Bulu. If they flapped, flopped, squeaked, or squawked, they were on his charge account. Their terrified cries thrilled him. But he never *caught* anything. That would have spoiled the fun.

Anna had reached her wit's end. She banished Bulu from all photo walks and grounded him at the house. So he started a new game. Escape artist. Whether squeezing through a partly open window, tunneling through the reed walls, or standing on his hind legs and wildly thrashing his paws at the latch till the door sprang open, Bulu inevitably found a way out. Anna had only one alternative. She got a lock.

Anna had walked about a mile on the riverbed when she spotted a goliath heron. It was about fifty yards ahead standing in a small pool. She looked through her binoculars and saw that it had just speared a catfish. To conceal herself, she set up under some thornbushes overlapping the embankment. She sat down in the sand, opened her knapsack, and pulled out the tripod.

As she attached the telephoto lens to the camera, high-pitched twittering sounds shattered the stillness. *CHURR CHURR CHURR CHURR.* Something had been disturbed. Anna stood up and was looking anxiously around when suddenly the bush exploded. A mob of banded mongooses dashed from the brush and scurried down the embankment, churring in panic, onto the riverbed. Then a white streak blurred past in hot pursuit of the terrified creatures. *RUFF RUFF RUFF RUFF.* Bulu hounded the band across the sand, then chased them one by one as the pack split.

Exasperated, Anna sat down. It was hopeless to try to call him off. She rested her back against the sandbank. *Perhaps he picked the lock this time,* she thought, watching Bulu and the scuttling gang, tails flying high, disappearing down the riverbed.

"We *could* keep him on a leash," Steve said as he sat at the supper table. "You'd have peace of mind. And Bulu would be safe."

"I suppose," Anna said, standing beside the stove. She lifted the kettle and thought a moment. "At least after dark he never tries to chase things or venture far from the house."

"That's true." Steve looked out the window at the fading light. "We know where he can be found every evening at sunset. At his spot under the mopane tree on the riverbank." He smiled. "Maybe he's waiting for the elephants to cross?" Steve got up, poured more tea from the pot, and headed for the door. "I think I'll join him."

Sitting on the embankment, Bulu was outlined against the red sky. He was facing the wide opening in the bank a few hundred feet away—the dried-up mouth of the Chowo tributary. Elephants often used the gap to enter the riverbed. During the dry season, sometimes over a hundred elephants from various herds crossed the sands at the same time. Bulu, hearing footsteps, turned his head.

"Sorry, old boy, it's just me. The birds have all gone to bed." Bulu made a little noise as he yawned. "A bit tuckered out, huh? Mongooses give you a workout?" Steve thought back to how a few months ago, Bulu had tried to chase some village chickens but ended up being chased by a rooster. From then on, Bulu gave all roosters respect—and he stopped chasing chickens. That misadventure now gave Steve an idea. What if he and Anna took Bulu on a safari far into the bush? Maybe Bulu could learn to respect wild animals the way he'd learned to respect chickens?

Steve sat on the embankment and took a long, hard look at Bulu. "It's time you start learning a few survival skills, big guy. You've got to anticipate which animals will run away from you . . . and which ones will run after you." Steve sipped his tea and breathed in the peppery scent of the Luangwa. "Maybe teaching you a little *discipline* will do the trick." He then put his arm around Bulu. "We can't put a leash on a free spirit. This is Africa."

"The workers have done an incredible job," Steve said to Anna, standing beside the cinder block foundation. The cement floor was perfectly smooth and level. The men were now laying the block walls, which had reached a three-foot height. "We're ahead of schedule." Steve beamed. "They've done all this in only three weeks."

"Think the roof will be up before the rainy season?" Anna asked.

"A good chance with these guys."

Grrrrrr. Bulu appeared beside them. He had spotted a squirrel walking along a log. But he didn't bother to go after it. Anna smiled. "Bulu doesn't like trespassers on *his* property."

"Bulu's bored with squirrels. Chasing them is beneath his dignity." Steve chuckled as he reached down to pet him. "Bulu, you will learn one lesson on our trek to-morrow. There are animals in the bush a lot more fero-cious than squirrels." He looked toward the Chowo riverbed to his left. "Should make for a most fascinating safari."

⟶

Six solid-nosed bullets, the size of marker pens, lay on the table inside the bush house. Steve loaded the cartridges into his bolt-action .458 Winchester Magnum rifle. If a shooter's aim was right, one solid-nosed bullet could drop a charging hippo or buffalo in its tracks. Steve was wary of aggressive bull hippos in the dry season. Despite its two-ton weight, a hippo could run flat out at twenty miles an hour. During territorial fights over lagoons, older bulls were driven out looking for new pools. Steve appreciated the crushing power of a hippo's massive jaws and teeth. He once saw the gruesome remains of a fisher-man who had been attacked by a hippo. The man's body had been chomped nearly in half.

Bulu paced at the door, sensing the excitement as Steve slung the rifle over his shoulder. He wore a backpack bulging with supplies, as did Anna. "Okay, Bulu. We're on safari," Steve announced, grabbing his binoculars.

"More like a field trip for unruly boys." Anna laughed as Bulu raced out the door.

Steve and Anna stepped outside into the early-morning light and headed for the Chowo. Reaching its banks, they stopped at the ten-foot-high cement bridge that was a lifeline during high rains. To their right, the dried-up stream led to the Luangwa. To their left, the Chowo looked like a sand highway leading into the bush. It was the path they planned to follow.

Steve unfolded an old surveyor's map. A squiggly line showed the Chowo disappearing into the Nchendeni Hills and beyond. He examined the map's details. "I don't see any springs marked. We'll need to be careful of our water." He folded up the map. "Let's stick to the riverbed. Too easy to get lost in the thickets."

They climbed down onto the sand and headed up its winding course. Bulu trotted along close beside.

For the first day of the two-day safari, Steve and Anna planned to hike several miles, then set up an overnight fly camp. They hoped the journey would teach Bulu to respect larger, more-powerful animals, just as he had learned to respect roosters. He needed to learn to quickly read a beast's intent in its body language—that there's an invisible line of animal boundaries that he must never cross. If he did, it could turn lethal.

The trek would also give Steve and Anna an opportunity to do some detective work. Were ivory or meat poachers operating farther up the Chowo? If there was a water hole to be found, the answer was most likely yes.

Steve and Anna plodded along, their feet sinking in the hot sand. Bulu walked much easier. The deep, narrow riverbed held heat like a radiator. A few hundred yards of hiking seemed like a hundred miles. The only sound was the monotonous whine of locust wings. After two hours, they came upon a tree lying across the riverbed, its roots torn from the bank during the summer floods. They took off their packs and rested under the trunk. Steve poured water from his canteen into a bowl for Bulu. A half hour later, the trio was back on their feet and trudging onward, Bulu sniffing at every stick and rock.

By mid-afternoon, the soaring heat ground the minutes into hours. The Chowo twisted, then turned back on itself, making the trek toward the hills seem endless. When a section of the riverbed eventually straightened, Bulu spotted something in the distance. It looked like flat black stones in the sand. He ran to inspect. "Buffalo," Steve said as they approached the black droppings. The dung was still moist on the surface. "Can't be too far from here." He examined the deep cloven-hoof prints, which revealed that there was only one animal. "A *kakuli* . . . an old bull." His gaze followed the tracks in the sand. He stood up and released the safety on the rifle. "Keep your eyes sharp." They continued walking as Bulu trotted in front of them.

Keeping his attention on the buffalo's prints, Steve thought of Mitch. He was grateful for the bush education he had gotten from him on many foot safaris. Steve vividly remembered Mitch's words of warning: *Never surprise a* kakuli. *I'd rather meet five hundred buff in a herd. They'll turn and move off. Not a* kakuli. *If he takes a disliking to you, he'll come after you like Attila the Hun . . . his meat-hook horns ripping out your guts like link sausages.* Steve looked ahead, relieved that the riverbed now ran straight, giving full visibility.

Bulu ran along snuffling the buffalo tracks. The prints diverted sharply to the left and up the embankment. He continued following them as they entered thick undergrowth. "Bulu!" Anna called. "No! Come back here!" A moment later, Bulu trotted back down the bank. Then he lifted his leg and peed on the buffalo dung. "Marking *your* territory?" Anna laughed, relieved he'd returned quickly. "Defending it won't be so easy."

By late afternoon, Steve and Anna were reaching the low point of their endurance. Anna stopped to take a swig of water and look around. "There's a winter thorn tree ahead." She pointed to the blue-green foliage above the brush. "Looks like a good place to camp for the night."

They climbed the sandy bank and walked toward the tree. Its towering branches covered them like an umbrella, offering the only shade in the otherwise naked woods. The winter thorn is one of the few trees in Luangwa to keep its foliage in the winter and drop its leaves in the summer. Steve and Anna took off their backpacks and plopped down. They opened their canteens and poured some water into a bowl. Bulu eagerly lapped it dry, then ran over to inspect some dried elephant droppings, peppered with winter thorn seeds. Anna leaned back against the tree trunk, mopping sweat with her bandanna. "Quite remarkable," she said. "Bulu's the only one who's not tired."

"So far, he gets an A for endurance."

Suddenly Bulu raised his head and stood completely still. He stared into the thorn thickets. Steve put his finger to his lips for silence. Just as Anna looked toward the bushes, Bulu bolted and disappeared into the undergrowth. *RUFF RUFF RUFF RUFF.* Steve grabbed his rifle and rushed to follow but was blocked by the impenetrable thorns. *Ruff ruff ruff ruff ruff.* The barking became fainter and fainter.

"*Bulu! Bulu!*" Anna yelled, jumping to her feet. They

stood listening. There was a slight rustling noise. Then a flash of movement in the brush. Something was coming straight at them! A blur of horns, hooves, stripes, and white tail ran through the clearing and then vanished into another thicket. It was a three-foot-high adult bushbuck.

Steve and Anna looked back into the thorn labyrinth. "*Bulu?*" Anna called. "*Bulu?*" Silence. Her heart pounding, she then saw something white moving through the branches. Bulu was slowly working his way out and emerged into the open. "Bulu!" Anna cried, dropping to her knees and hugging him. He was covered with small cuts and scratches on his chest. He yawned and wagged his tail, looking very pleased with himself. Steve let out a sigh as he lowered his rifle. "You get an A-plus in scaring us half to death and an F in stalking and tracking."

Steve knelt down to open his backpack. He pulled out a small folded tent and removed the camping supplies. "I'll get the fire going," he said, spotting fallen limbs and branches scattered around.

"And *you*," Anna scolded Bulu as she dabbed water on his scratches, "are grounded to the tent—before you give us both heart attacks."

A slice of moon hung in the sky. The Chowo bush had become a world of shadows. The still air vibrated with thousands of night insects. Steve and Anna were fast asleep in the tent, ventilated with mesh windows and a zipped-up screen door. Bulu, lying between them, had fallen asleep on his back with paws folded over his chest. A small stream of smoke rose from the dying flames of the campfire.

There was a faint chuffing sound in the distance, like the sawing of wood. Bulu stirred a moment but did not wake. A couple of minutes later, a phantom appeared on the edge of the riverbank. Like a shadow, he moved across the open space, heading straight for the tent. His silhouette was unmistakable. Wide head, square shoulders, stocky legs, fat tail curving upward toward his back. He sensed the presence of life inside. He moved closer. The smoke and hot embers in the fire stopped him. His yellow eyes stared into the mesh, alert for any movement. The smoke dulled his keen sense of smell. He looked toward the riverbed. Seemingly indecisive, he returned his gaze to the tent. He stood there for a moment longer, watching. Then he turned, padded along the bank, and disappeared up the riverbed.

———

Whaag-hoo whaag-hoo. A flashlight flicked on inside the tent. Bulu was instantly on his feet, alert at the mesh door. Steve and Anna sat up and listened to the sound in the distance. *WHAAG-hoo WHAAG-hoo.* Frantic barking echoed down the riverbank. It was the alarm call of a troop of baboons. Anna held Bulu back as Steve grabbed his rifle and crawled outside. He stood in front of the campfire ashes and listened—*ree ree ree ree ree*— to the rhythm of insect songs. He shone his flashlight into the underbrush, then up into the trees, looking for reflecting eyes. Nothing. He pointed the beam downward and was alarmed at what he saw. "Come have a look," he said, stooping down for closer scrutiny. "We had company at our doorstep."

Anna peered out the tent and looked at the tracks. "Leopard!" She held Bulu tighter.

Steve followed the footprints to the bank and swept a spot of light along the sand. He saw that the leopard

had headed upstream. "We'll keep an eye on his tracks," he said, returning to the tent. "Let's pack up now so we can leave at first light."

A pale pink dawn backlit the trees as Steve and Anna shouldered their packs. Bulu was already waiting on the bank. They stepped down into the riverbed to find that the night air had cooled the sand. As the sun rose, the trio walked along silently, focused on the leopard's tracks. Bulu kept his nose close to the ground. A half mile farther along, Steve noticed another set of tracks overlapping the cat's. "Lucky day for mother warthog," he said, pointing out her prints and those of her youngsters. "Her babies missed getting eaten." Eventually the leopard tracks led up the embankment and into the woods. The trio continued along the riverbed.

By noon, the sun scorched the landscape. Steve and Anna reached a wide curve in the dried river. Bulu abruptly stopped and held his nose to the air. He walked on a little farther and sniffed again. Then he ran off and disappeared around the crook of the embankment. "Bulu—come back here!" Steve and Anna rushed after him. But after a couple of minutes, the deeper sand and the weight of backpacks slowed their pace to a slog.

They stopped to listen. "I don't hear him," Anna said. "He always barks when he's after something."

As they reached the outward curve of the embankment, Bulu suddenly came bounding back toward them. "Bulu!" Anna shouted. "*Bad* dog! *Baaad.*" She had started to give him a good bawling out when they noticed something strange. His feet and muzzle were *wet.* "So *that's* what he smelled."

They walked around the sandbank and were happily surprised to find a water hole the size of a small pond. A low depression in the riverbed contained a pool about six inches deep. Steve noticed grooves in the ground where elephants had used their tusks to dig. Clear water sifted up through the sand. Bulu walked into the puddle to cool off and drink, then checked out the mosaic of animal tracks coming and going. "Quite a meeting place," Anna said. "Hyenas, genet cats, warthogs, buffalo, a honey badger." Dried elephant droppings were scattered about like hay, broken up by the monkeys that had picked out undigested seeds. Bulu sniffed the dung. "Old news, Bulu. Those elephants haven't been here in days."

Bulu followed some prints and trotted along the riverbed. He then stopped, looked up at the embankment, and held his nose to the air. He seemed to take a particular interest in something and ran up the steep slope. "Get *baack* here!" Anna called. Bulu hesitated in front of the thorn brush. He stood there as though frozen, white tail up, head straight forward. "Not another bushbuck," Anna said, watching him from the base of the bank. But there was something about his behavior now that began to spook her. Bulu didn't bark or run—but made a long, low guttural growl. She silently signaled to Steve, who was walking up behind her.

Steve set down his backpack and unshouldered his rifle. Then he trod softly up the embankment. Bulu was still riveted in place. Steve walked over to stand beside him, checked the bolt on his rifle, and listened. His eyes tried to probe between the entangled thorns. He looked to his left and saw what appeared to be an opening in the brush. Stepping carefully between brittle twigs, he approached the gap. Peering in for a better look, he saw the tracks of antelope. But farther up the narrow path, he noticed deep depressions in the sand. Strangely, the tracks stopped fifty feet from the opening. His suspicions aroused, he decided to enter the thorn tunnel. He signaled to Anna to hold on to the dog. She climbed the bank and knelt down and put her arms around Bulu. She was alarmed when Steve disappeared into the underbrush. Whatever he might have spotted, he could easily get trapped in the stabbing thorns if an animal attacked.

Hampered by his rifle, Steve crouched down to enter the small bramble path. As if untangling barbed wire, he picked aside the thorns that clawed at his sweat-soaked shirt. Scratches and small beads of blood peppered his arms and legs as he continued to work his way toward the large tracks. Determined to reach the prints, Steve pushed himself forward in the bramble. Suddenly they were at his feet. It was what he suspected. *Boot tracks.* He hunkered down to get a better look.

The footprints were fresh. A man wandering in such a remote area meant only one thing—a poacher. Steve stared ahead into the narrow path but could not detect any movement. He listened. But the only sound was the high-pitched hum of locusts. Steve knew one thing for sure. Someone had been there recently and might have seen them. He slowly turned around and stooped back along the path of thorns.

Anna handed Steve the canteen as he reappeared from the bushes. "A man's footprints," Steve said quietly. "We may have scared him off. Don't know if Bulu saw someone or picked up a lingering scent. But I want to check it out."

"Steve, you know a poacher seldom travels alone." She grasped his arm. "I'll come with you."

"You'll need to stay here to hold on to Bulu." Steve looked along the riverbed to where an elephant trail had worn down the embankment into a shallow slope. He gulped some water, then turned and walked the fifty yards toward it. Reaching the place, he saw that it was a wide trail disappearing into the brush. The herds had worn a path as smooth as a tarmac road. He turned onto it. Buffalo dung was spread about like a minefield. He looked uneasily toward the curve in the path. He knew a *kakuli* would not share the road. Several yards farther on, he spotted them—boot prints on top of elephant tracks. He noticed what looked like cuts on small branches. He stooped for a closer look and peered into the bushes. A flash of metal. It was a small coil of wire the size of a lariat. He walked farther down the path and found another coil. Seeing more cut branches on the opposite side, he spied three more wires. The elephant trail had been turned into snare alley.

Steve pulled the hunting knife from his belt and slashed the wires free from the bushes. Farther down, the path opened up into a small clearing. A faint smoky smell caught his attention. He walked over to investigate. Under a stunted tree, the ends of half-burned logs had been reduced to smoldering ashes. The remains of a fly camp. Steve found five different sets of boot prints between the flattened stubbles of dry grass. He scoured the ground. Then he noticed something in the powdery dust. A faint imprint where a poacher had laid down a rifle. It was a homemade muzzle-loading barrel with a rough wooden stock. He sifted through the sand and found bits of metal. They were shrapnel, pieces of scrap iron, used as bullets to kill larger game like buffalo and elephants. Concerned about Anna, he gripped his rifle and retraced his steps to the riverbed.

Leaning up against the backpacks under the thin shade of a bush, Anna waited anxiously. Bulu saw Steve walking back and raced off to greet him. Anna got up. "You had me worried!"

"I found the remains of a poachers' camp. Five of 'em. They've run off. Campfire still smoldering." Steve held up the snares. "They're using muzzle loaders. Lucky we didn't surprise them on the riverbed. I doubt they'd hesitate to shoot." He looked at Bulu and knelt down beside him. "Good boy. Looks like we've got more than just a watchdog here. This dog can *think*." Steve scratched Bulu behind his ears. "For a while there, I thought you had no common sense." Bulu wagged his tail, then yawned with a little yowl of pleasure. Steve stood up. "You know something, Anna? Bulu restrained every urge to chase whatever he saw or smelled in the brush—even suppressed his barking. He seemed to sense a greater danger to us."

Anna smiled. She thought back to when she worried about Bulu's being different.

"We don't want to hang around here." Steve picked up the snares and tied them to his backpack. "It's too late to reach home now. We'll need to camp farther down the riverbed. Less chance of anyone spotting our fire." He looked in his pack. "Four cans of juice. How're we doing on water?"

"Five full canteens."

Steve glanced at the sun lowering behind the trees. "We'll be doing some walking in the dark." He hoisted up his backpack. "Let's try to keep Bulu close."

Steve and Anna stepped up their pace to take advantage of the waning light. Bulu trotted closely beside them down the center of the riverbed. They continued to watch the embankments for a possible campsite, but the thorn brush choked out any open space. They trudged onward.

Camping in the riverbed was out of the question. It was too much of a pathway for creatures of the night. Dusk is fleeting in Africa, and the woodlands were fading into shadow. The dim light played tricks on their imaginations. That black object up against the bank *must* be a buffalo. It appeared to move. Steve stopped and clicked his flashlight onto the figure. But the buffalo was an uprooted tree stump. Bulu was not so easily fooled. He trotted along keeping alert to any *real* animals that might be lurking around the bend.

The stars slowly began to light the sky. At a place where the riverbed widened out to about two hundred feet, Steve aimed his beam at an embankment. It jutted out like the prow of a ship. On top there might be open ground.

They climbed the bank and happily found enough room for a tent and campfire. The overhang would give them a good vantage point to spot any movement in the riverbed. While Anna prepared to set up the tent, Steve turned his flashlight into the wall of brush to search for firewood. He was always wary of snakes at night, especially spitting cobras. If threatened, one will instantly rise up, spread its hood, and spit venom, aiming for the eyes. The poison can cause permanent blindness. As a precaution, Steve threw a couple of sticks into the brush. Then he collected scattered driftwood, left over from the summer floods. The hardwood mopane logs would burn long into the night. He laid the firewood into a small pile. As he struck a match, a dark stone in the dirt caught his attention. He reached down and picked it up. It was a piece of flint. He switched on his flashlight to examine it closer.

"Anna," he called. "You've got to see this!" She hurried up to him. "Looks like a flint tool," he said, turning it over and over in his fingers. "Could be part of a Middle Stone Age spearhead."

Anna smiled as she watched him examine each facet on the flint like a delighted kid. Steve had a passion for paleontology and a scholarly interest in fossils and pre-historic life-forms in the valley.

Anna sat down beside her backpack and dug out her Swiss Army knife. She opened a tin of corned beef. Bulu ran up to her with his tail wagging in anticipation. Corned beef was one of his favorites. As she scraped the can into his bowl, Bulu practically inhaled his supper. He was so hungry that Anna had to open another can. After licking his lips, Bulu sat and waited for her to get out the hard bread. She held it out for him, but he hesitated. "How could I forget, Bulu?" Anna chuckled. She then opened a tin of butter and spread it on the bread. It was a special treat that Bulu expected every day. "Do you think he'll leave any for us?" Steve laughed as he stoked the fire. "He never lets us forget the butter."

The flames died out as the logs burned slowly into red-hot pokers. Anna cleaned the tin plates with sand as Steve poured steaming coffee into cups. "Safari blend. Includes the grounds and anything that's drowned in the pot." Steve grinned as he added sugar to the cups. "Now let's move to the living room and turn on the stars."

Anna stood up and walked with Steve to the edge of

the overhang. Bulu followed and sat on his haunches. Steve and Anna never ceased to be stunned by the sheer number of stars in the African sky. The Milky Way electrified the heavens as if all the city lights of the world had been switched on at once. Tens of thousands of stars seemed to rain down like a meteor shower, snagging onto the bushes and trees. The Southern Cross hung above the woodlands as though illuminated for a light show.

Anna turned her attention to Bulu. He was looking upward. "Steve . . . have you ever wondered if animals really *think* about their surroundings? If they have . . . *an awareness* about life?"

"I doubt if Bulu will ever be an Oxford philosopher," Steve laughed. "Though I wonder if he has a sense of awe. The way he goes off every evening on his own to sit by himself on the bank. Watching the sun go down. Even looking up at the night sky." He took a swig of coffee. "How could that be instinct?"

Anna thought a moment. "I think people sometimes use instinct as a cop-out term. A way to demean animals. Like they're just robots that can't think or feel."

Steve nodded and smiled. "Humans don't like being humbled."

A wedge of moon rose above the trees. Steve and Anna had already rolled out their sleeping mats inside the tent. It was far too risky to sleep outside. The African night belongs to predators.

"Okay, Bulu. Time for bed." Anna beckoned as Bulu found his place between the mats. He turned in a circle, then lay down. Anna opened the vent and zipped down the mesh door as Steve clicked off his flashlight. Within minutes, they fell asleep, Bulu on his back, exhausted from the long day.

An hour later, Bulu awakened and stood up. Barely audible even to his keen ears was a familiar sound. He stepped toward the mesh door and listened. *Aaaaar . . . uummmmph . . . aaaaar . . . uummmmph . . . aaaaar . . . uummmmph.* He sensed the sound was very far off. Then he heard it behind him, the same sound, low and in the distance. *Aaaaar . . . uummmmph . . . aaaaar . . . uummmmph . . . aaaaar . . . uummmmph.* The calls continued a few moments longer, then ceased. Bulu turned around and lay down between Steve and Anna. He rested his muzzle on his paws, eyes open, and listened through the night.

Steve woke at dawn. He was poking the ashes to relight the campfire when he noticed something out of the corner of his eye. Across the riverbed, a small animal on the far bank slipped behind a driftwood tree. It moved so fast that he couldn't make out what it was. He thought nothing of it and added branches to the fire. Then he turned his head and was surprised to see Bulu behind him, staring intensely across the riverbed. Steve glanced at the tent and saw where the dog had slipped through the half-zipped mesh. Bulu started to growl.

Steve looked to the riverbed and his heart jumped. Forty or so small animals in single file were moving down the far bank. It was a troop of vervet monkeys! Before Steve could get to his feet, Bulu launched himself from the bank like a greyhound at a starting gate. He was a white streak kicking up sand, heading on a collision course with the monkeys.

Caught off guard and in the open, the vervets stopped and stood up on their hind legs. With their dark human-like faces, jaws dropped, eyes blinking rapidly, they looked astonished. What was this strange creature? As the dog barreled toward them, they scattered in every direction squealing like pigs. *EEEEEEEEEE*

EEEEEEEEEE EEEEEEEEEE. Bulu barked furiously as he targeted one small monkey and chased it crazily around in circles. But a few of the bigger males suddenly turned back, flashed their long, sharp canines, and ran straight toward the dog. *AAAAARR AAAAARR AAAAARR AAAAARR.* Bulu stopped in his tracks. These monkeys were now coming after *him*!

"BULU!" Anna raced out of the tent, hearing the uproar.

Steve was already halfway across the riverbed, bellowing, *"BULU! COME BACK!"*

Bulu just stood there, seemingly bewildered. The aggressive males stopped within a few feet of the dog, screaming and hissing threats, baring their teeth. Bulu then lost his nerve—and started running *back* across the riverbed, triggering the males to chase him. But when the monkeys suddenly spotted two humans racing toward them, they panicked and turned tail.

"*BAAD* DOG! *BAAD* BULU!" Steve and Anna rushed over to restrain him.

EEEEEEEEEEEEEE. A mass exodus of monkeys was streaming along the far embankment and scrambling up the trees. Then, like outraged tenants peering down from their apartments, the vervets were screeching, spitting, and hissing verbal abuse from the highest branches—trying to regain their lost dignity.

Steve and Anna held Bulu tight.

Knowing he was now safe, Bulu barked back a volume of his own insults.

The sun had just appeared above the treetops as Steve opened a can of fruit juice. Bulu lay next to Anna, peering up at Steve, who spoke sternly. "If we had a doghouse, Bulu, you'd be in it." Bulu turned sheepishly from the scolding, put his head down on his paws, and closed his eyes.

"Maybe we're expecting too much. He's only a year old," said Anna. "But he did learn *something* on this safari. He learned how to size up just about every situation. Especially sensing the danger from a human presence yesterday. And we learned something too."

"That Bulu has bravado?" Steve looked across the riverbed, where monkeys were still perched in the trees, nattering and chattering.

"Yes, there's that, of course. But more important— he's learning when to back off in a confrontation."

Steve thought a moment, then put his hand on Bulu's head. Immediately Bulu got to his feet, wagged his tail, and yawned. "Okay, big guy," said Steve softly. "I guess you've learned that *some* games can turn deadly. There's one survival law of the bush you mustn't forget: *Never let your guard down.* If you do, the bush will be very unforgiving."

Steve and Anna trekked down the riverbed. They had kept a steady march ever since breaking camp hours earlier. Bulu trotted along tirelessly beside them. They rested every so often for water breaks under the stingy shade of thornbushes. By late afternoon, they spotted the cement bridge ahead. "Home turf, Bulu!" Anna announced. *Ruff ruff ruff ruff.*

"Go for it, Bulu!" Steve cheered. This set Bulu off in a frenzy of excitement, running around them in circles. "Go, Bulu. *Go!*" *RUFF RUFF RUFF RUFF.* "GO, BULU. *GO!*" The louder Steve and Anna laughed and clapped, the louder Bulu barked and the faster he ran. They had incited what they called a Bulu crazy spell.

A few minutes later, Steve and Anna reached the bridge and climbed the embankment. Nearing the construction site, they saw the African workers huddled together, chattering excitedly. Something had interrupted their jobs. Mabvuto, one of the young men, spotted

Steve and Anna and ran toward them. "Mister Steve. Miss Anna. Lions are here! *Baby* lions."

"Where?" Steve plopped down his backpack.

"Not far." Mabvuto pointed toward the river. "Three babies. We saw them under a bush near the river."

"Show me the place, Mabvuto." Steve shot an anxious glance at Anna as he unshouldered his rifle. "Their mother's going to be close by."

"Bulu!" Anna called as she saw him walking toward the workers. "You're going inside the house *now*."

Steve knew he'd need to use soft-nosed bullets for lions because they spread on impact. A first shot might stop a charge. One thing was for sure. Mama Lion wasn't going to be real happy to see him. He emptied the hard-nosed bullets from his rifle chamber and replaced them. He stuffed extra cartridges into the bullet loops on his belt. "Mabvuto, stay close to me. If anything moves in the bushes, stand still. Don't run."

Gripping his Winchester, Steve strode toward the river with Mabvuto behind him. There was not a hint of a breeze to test the wind. Fortunately, the dry stubble gave good ground visibility. Mabvuto pointed to three acacia trees at the riverbank, where the cubs had been discovered. Steve worried that the adult lions could be resting out of sight below the embankment. If disturbed with the cubs nearby, the pride would attack. He remembered what Mitch had told him on safari: *Nothing can move faster from a standing position than a charging lion. It can cover a hundred feet of ground in three seconds.* It was a fact not lost on Steve as he neared the embankment. Mabvuto suddenly tapped him on the shoulder and pointed at a thornbush between the trees. Steve stopped and listened. A lion will sometimes growl a warning. But there was no sound. Slowly, Steve stepped closer to the bush and peered into the shade. There were three tiny animals lying flat against the earth. They were blackish gray with sparse hair—and shiny bald heads!

Steve gave a sigh of relief and put down the rifle. He started to laugh. "Mabvuto. These are not baby lions. They're baby *warthogs.*" Mabvuto looked down and started to laugh. When Steve walked closer to the warthogs, one panicked and ran off. "Try to catch it!" he yelled, and Mabvuto raced after it. Steve stood still so as not to scare the others. It gave him a moment to observe them. Because warthogs give birth at the end of the dry season, Steve estimated the piglets to be about three weeks old. Mother warthogs would never abandon their young. Most likely a lion had caught the mother off guard and killed her. Steve knew the piglets would die within hours from dehydration. He decided to rescue them. As he stepped closer, the piglets pressed themselves flatter to the ground. Steve knelt down slowly, then with both hands grasped them. They made little squeaking noises in fear. Holding them gently, he walked back home.

Minutes later, Steve reached the house. "Anna, come and meet the 'lion cubs'!"

Anna quickly opened the door. Startled, she tried to comprehend what Steve was holding.

"*Warthogs.*" Steve laughed. "The workers had a case of mistaken identity."

"But . . . where's the mother?"

"No trace of her. Probably lions."

"Oh no." Anna looked at the helpless piglets.

"There were three. One ran off and Mabvuto went after it." Steve handed the piglets over to Anna. "Don't know how long they've been in the grass."

Anna cuddled them close. "Steve, their little bodies are burning up!"

"We've got to get some milk into them," Steve said, hurrying into the house.

"I'll cool them down with wet towels," Anna said, following. She put the piglets on the floor and they immediately flattened themselves. Then they spotted Bulu.

He was walking slowly toward them and he was deadly quiet. These two intruders were in *Bulu's* house! He moved as though stalking them. When he was within a couple of feet of them, he stopped. He sniffed the air, then quickly ran at the piglets and started to lick them all over. The babies opened their eyes, seeming to relax. They got to their feet and started to sniff Bulu.

"Well, will you look at that." Steve shook his head. "Bulu's charmed the babies."

"And he didn't try to chase them," Anna said, looking dumbfounded.

Steve stood at the table mixing powdered milk with water. He reached up to a shelf and opened a box and took out two medicine droppers. He handed one to Anna. They sat down on the floor and picked up the babies. Anna put the milk-filled end to the mouth of one piglet as Steve did the same to the other. The babies instantly sucked the droppers dry. Bulu walked over, sat down on his haunches, and watched. After a few minutes, the babies began to fart loudly. The more milk, the more gas. Bulu cocked his head at the piglets' amazing variety of rude tunes and toots.

A short while later, the babies had had their fill and fallen asleep. Anna held them up and looked underneath. "Well, they're both females."

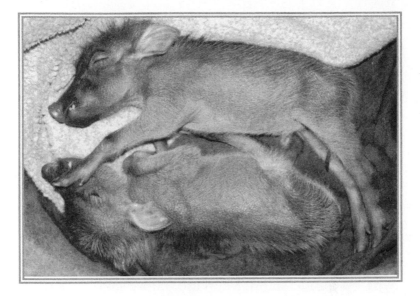

"What can we name them?" Steve asked.

Anna studied their piglike faces, baby tusks, and tiny hooves like miniature high-heeled shoes. She thought a moment, then smiled. "Pinky and Perky!"

"Yes," Steve laughed. "Like the piggy puppets on British TV."

Anna looked around the room. "Now, where are Pinky and Perky going to sleep?"

"Bulu's old basket will work." Steve fetched the basket and lined it with towels. He set it down beside the piglets.

Anna picked up the babies and placed them snugly

inside. "Perfect." She then got up and put the bed beside the watercooler.

As Steve started to wash the medicine droppers, Mabvuto appeared in the doorway. "Mister Steve." He spoke quietly. "I look everywhere. Men help me too. We not find baby warthog. I very sorry."

Steve thought a moment as he gazed out the window. The sun was low behind the trees across the river. The approaching darkness would make further search impossible. Steve caught Anna's eye and they nodded. They knew the runaway piglet would not survive the night. "We understand, Mabvuto," Steve said. "You tried your best."

———

Faint light from the waxing moon shone through the window. Steve and Anna had crashed into bed hours earlier, soon after sunset. They had been completely wiped out from the long, strenuous day.

Just before first light of dawn, Anna got up to get a drink. She walked over to the watercooler and looked down at the piglets' basket. It was empty! She looked toward the door. It was tightly shut. She quickly peeked behind the shower wall. She stood there a moment trying to comprehend in the dim light. Then she tiptoed over to the dining table and lit a lantern. She went over to the bed and gently woke Steve. As he opened his eyes, Anna put her finger to her lips for silence. He was a bit groggy, and it took him a moment to wake. She beckoned him to follow. Quietly, they walked across the room and peered into the shower stall. Steve beamed. Anna leaned her head against his shoulder. There was Bulu in his usual sleeping position on his back. Resting on his belly were the two little piglets, sound asleep.

"**W**atch out for crocs in the pools," Steve said, grabbing the coffeepot from the stove. "You know how distracted you get when taking pictures."

"I'll keep my eyes open," Anna promised, sitting on the floor feeding the piglets. Bulu sat next to her watching the babies with intense interest. It was his morning routine ever since the warthogs arrived a couple of weeks ago. "Pinky and Perky need some exercise outside. They've got a little diarrhea."

"Probably the milk we're giving them," Steve said. "We know *nothing* about raising warthogs."

"What about Mitch? Didn't he once take care of orphaned animals?" Anna asked. "We could get his advice."

"I don't know if he's ever raised warthogs." Steve took a gulp of coffee. "When I get to the work site, I'll send Mabvuto off on his bike with a note." He picked up the blueprints and headed out.

A half hour later, Anna finished stuffing a satchel with her lunch, canteens, two cameras, binocs, and a portable tripod. She also packed powdered milk to mix up for the piglets. Bulu walked over to the door as Pinky and Perky followed him. Anna stepped outside and walked to the riverbank. The dawn had just brushed the trees with orange light. She stood a moment on the bank scanning the riverbed, then climbed down onto the sandy floor. Bulu paced on ahead as Pinky and Perky trailed closely behind. Anna laughed to herself thinking of her friends back in England walking their dogs. If they could only see her now—walking the warthogs!

She planned to trek a couple of miles downstream to photograph carmine bee-eaters. During the dry season, these rose-colored insect-eating birds flocked by the thousands to excavate nests in the sandy riverbanks.

The cool morning sand made the walk invigorating. Bulu trotted along with Pinky and Perky. About a mile farther along, Bulu stopped and sniffed the air. Anna picked up her binoculars and saw what caught his attention. A small muddy pool near a bend in the riverbed. A few minutes later, they reached the shrinking water hole. It was only about twenty-five feet across and barely two inches deep. To Anna's surprise, Pinky and Perky beat Bulu to the water. They waded in and immediately plunked down in the mud. Bulu splashed in

after them. It appeared as though a game had started. The tiny warthogs turned over on their backs and began to wallow and squeak with delight.

Anna laughed. The piglets looked like overturned

windup toys with mechanical legs held straight in the air, scissoring back and forth. Their friskiness and squeals incited a Bulu crazy spell. He began to run around and around the mud hole. *RUFF RUFF RUFF RUFF.* The louder Anna laughed, the faster Bulu ran, stopping periodically to bark at Pinky and Perky, who continued to wallow. Anna laughed so hard she had to sit down to catch her breath. And then, like their batteries had died, Pinky and Perky suddenly stopped and turned themselves upright.

Red streaks flitted over Anna's head. She looked up to see several carmine bee-eaters flying low above the riverbed. Then they flew along the top of the bank hunting for bees. Bulu came over and nudged her. He was ready to move. She got up and continued walking. A mile or so farther along, the riverbed widened to reveal a panoramic view of the Luangwa. To the southeast, she could see the tips of the distant blue hills of Mozambique. Sand the color of burnished copper lay like a carpet across the riverbed. The sweeping fifteen-foot-high embankments were pockmarked with nesting holes. Dazzling like hundreds of rubies tossed in the wind, the bee-eaters flitted in and out of their nests. Bulu stood silently and watched the frenetic activity but did not bother the tiny birds.

Anna opened her satchel, took out the larger camera, and attached the telephoto lens. Bulu sat down on his haunches beside her. The warthogs lay beside him and went to sleep. Anna was so distracted by the birds that she didn't pay much attention to the deep crescent-shaped water hole about a thousand feet farther along. If she had used her binoculars, she would have seen a suspicious object the size of a fallen log at its edge. Neglecting to check it out would soon prove a terrifying mistake.

Anna fastened the camera to the swivel tripod. She put her eye to the viewfinder and panned both banks for the best shot. When she focused the telephoto, she saw a herd of tangerine-colored puku antelope standing on the left bank. Strangely, they were all facing the same way, frozen as sculptures, staring down at something in the riverbed. She was just about to look at what they were watching when birds flew across the viewfinder. Wanting to capture the bee-eaters in mid-flight, she adjusted the camera settings and started clicking away. As the birds flew close to the bank, each one instantly found its own nest among the hundreds. Anna wondered how they could eat bees, wasps, and hornets with no ill effects. She planned to display the photos at the wildlife center to teach how birds are crucial to

Luangwa's ecosystem. Without some avian species, insects would quickly overpopulate.

When Anna swiveled her camera back to the left bank, she saw the puku herd still motionless, staring down into the riverbed. She turned the camera and zoomed in to see what had captured their attention. It was the crescent-shaped water hole. The green-mottled log at its edge had spiky scales—*and was moving*. It was a twelve-foot crocodile! She stepped back from the camera and peered down at her feet. Bulu and the piglets were gone. She looked around and spotted them in the center of the riverbed about two hundred feet away. They were heading straight for the water hole!

Anna had to think fast. If she started to chase after them, Bulu might think it a game and run. But if she walked at a brisk pace, she just might catch up with him in time. Bulu was still unaware of the crocodile. Anna quickened her stride. Bulu stopped a moment and sat down to scratch. This gave her precious seconds to close the gap. If she could just get within a few feet of Bulu, she would run and grab him. She knew she had only one chance.

Bulu got up and sniffed the sand. Anna stepped up her pace, desperately resisting the urge to run. Slowly, the gap closed. Anna paced within thirty, then twenty feet of Bulu and the piglets. The water hole lay barely a hundred feet ahead. Then Bulu suddenly halted. He put his nose to the air and stood dead still. The piglets stopped instantly. Bulu had smelled the croc. He started his long, low growl. Anna knew what that meant—it was now or never. She ran flat out. When Bulu looked back and saw Anna coming, he seemed to take it as a signal. He shot forward to charge the crocodile. "NOOO, BULU. *NOOO!!!*" Anna screamed. The crocodile turned its head slightly. Alarmed, it slithered along the mud, slipped into the pool, and submerged. A few seconds later, Bulu reached the edge of the water. He started barking frantically. Anna reached him and grabbed him around the waist. She looked up and saw the crocodile resurfacing fifty feet away, its cold raptor eyes staring at her. Shaking almost uncontrollably, she swept up Bulu in her arms and quickly distanced herself from the water hole. She was too weak, too winded, her mouth too dry to bawl him out.

Anna looked behind her and saw that the warthogs were still frozen in place. Then it occurred to her. Bulu had growled a warning for them to stop. He'd always been extremely wary of crocodiles, giving them a wide berth on the riverbanks. Bulu had become fiercely protective of the piglets—otherwise, Anna believed, he would not have risked confronting an animal he so feared.

Steve was helping one of the workers lift a cinder block onto a half-finished wall when Mitch's Land Rover rumbled up the driveway. Sitting beside him was Mabvuto, his bicycle stashed on the roof. The battered truck stopped in a gust of dust and Mitch stepped out. "Mabvuto tells me you've adopted a couple of warthogs."

"Actually, I think *Bulu* adopted them." Steve laughed as he shook hands. "Anna and he are out taking them for a walk."

"Speaking of Bulu, I've got some information for you on the drug used to treat sleeping sickness—the tryps—in dogs."

Steve nodded and grabbed a thermos and biscuit tin from the worktable. "Let's have a cold drink." He motioned Mitch toward the gazebo. "I want to pick your brain about warthogs too."

Moments later, they sat in safari chairs in the gazebo. "The drug's called berenil," Mitch explained. "It either kills or cures an infected animal. It's a poison, actually."

"*Poison?*"

"Yes. A small dose kills the trypanosome parasites. But too much kills the patient."

"How will I know if Bulu's infected?"

"When a *terrier* has no energy, sleeps all the time, and has an extremely high temperature, you'll know something's wrong. If they start walking around in circles, the disease is progressing fast. The parasite has gone to the brain. Remember, tsetse flies carry the tryps and there's no shortage of them in the valley." He reached into his shirt pocket for a notepad, tore off a piece of paper, and handed it to Steve. "There's a veterinary clinic in Chipata. It's not much of a hospital. But when the dog gets infected, it's critical you get him there at once. Without a berenil injection, he will *not* recover."

"Okay, Doc," Steve said. "Now tell me what you know about warthogs. We've been feeding the piglets powdered milk, and they usually have diarrhea."

"I raised one once," Mitch said. "It had the same problem at first. Microbes in the water mixed with the powder caused the diarrhea. You must use canned UHT-brand milk. It's boiled at an ultrahigh temperature that kills all the bacteria." He poured more tea from the thermos. "I made the mistake of getting too attached to my warthog. She followed me everywhere. But lions got her one night. Dug her right out of her burrow. I was very upset." He thought a moment as he added sugar to his cup. "You'll need to build a strong burrow. Lion-proof."

Steve gestured toward the construction site and smiled. "We've got plenty of cement."

"I've learned that orphaned animals need to be introduced to the bush gradually. It gives them the experience, on a daily basis, to learn to use their senses. Teaches them not to fear everything that moves, but rather to recognize the real dangers." He grabbed a biscuit from the tin and dunked it in his tea. "Every kid needs a mentor to show them the way. Otherwise, we'd all be hiding forever in our burrows."

"Speaking of kids . . ." Steve smiled as Anna suddenly appeared on the bank a hundred feet away.

Mitch leaned forward and squinted his pale blue eyes into the sun. He observed Bulu climbing the bank with the tiny warthogs, one on each side of him. When Bulu stopped to look around, the piglets stopped to look around. When Bulu trotted onward, the piglets trotted onward. Mitch raised his white bushy eyebrows. "Well, I'll be." He put down his cup. "Bulu's become a daddy."

Hummph *hummph hummph.* Hippos were grunting in the river in front of the house. They had come back from the lagoons as rain gradually began to refill the Luangwa. Every day, the clouds would build and loom over the Muchinga Escarpment, unleashing sudden downpours into the valley. Although the river was still only a few feet deep, its level rose by inches every day. Vegetation had sprouted along the riverbanks, attracting great numbers of hippos. It was December, and the rainy season had returned in force.

Fat raindrops made pockmarks in the soggy sand around the construction site. Wood scaffolding hugged the completed outer walls. Steve and the African workers stood on a platform nailing down tin roof sheeting on crossbeams. Jagged blades of lightning slashed through towering thunderclouds, causing them to hemorrhage over the Nchendeni Hills. Torrents of water came surging down the Chowo. Steve rested a moment to marvel at how the valley was transformed in only a month. One minute brown as a desert, the next green as an English summer. Lemon-yellow and jade leaves had popped open on the acacia and mopane trees. Grass shoots had exploded throughout the woodlands. It was as though the Luangwa had been resurrected.

Tak tak tak tak tak tak. A moment later, the door of the house opened. Anna stepped out wearing her slicker and a camera bag over her shoulder. She had heard the rapid-fire calls of a white-headed plover coming from the embankment. *Tak tak tak tak tak tak.* She headed off in the mist toward the river to locate the noisy bird. Bulu walked out with Pinky and Perky tailing him. The warthogs had grown to over half his size. They were fattening up fast on the lush vegetation. Bulu trotted on ahead of Anna, his attention focused on the ground. When he reached the bank's edge, he froze. The warthogs stopped behind him. Then Bulu slowly turned his head to the side, as though trying not to look at something.

Anna cautiously reached the overhang. A lone bull hippo, the size of a boulder, was standing only five feet below her! It rolled its yellow eyes upward in its huge protruding sockets. Its pinkish brown skin was glistening wet. Clumps of grass were sticking out of its closed mouth. Its eyes were locked on Anna. She held her breath and stood still, diverting her gaze from its stare. Her muscles tensed, ready for flight. She slowly backed away from the edge. Seeing Anna move, Bulu turned and slunk off. Anna backed up until she was out of the hippo's sight. Then she grabbed Bulu in her arms and hurriedly walked back to the house, the warthogs right behind her. Clutching Bulu tight, she felt his heart pulsing wildly. He was trembling all over in a shiver of fear.

By mid-morning, the mist had lifted and shafts of sunlight broke through the clouds. "Teatime!" Steve called on the scaffolding for a break. The workers had started to put down their hammers when Mabvuto pointed to something below. Steve looked down and saw three shadows racing together under the scaffolding, then out onto the open ground. It was Bulu, Pinky, and Perky.

The cool air had energized Bulu to start his favorite cut-to-the-chase game. Bulu was finding out just how fast warthogs can move. Pinky and Perky were giving the dog a run for his money. Steve and the workers watched the game as the warthogs squealed, outrunning Bulu, who hounded furiously after them. Bulu had one trick up his sleeve, however. The warthogs might run faster, but no one could *dodge* faster than Bulu. Not even a vervet. Bulu ran this way and that, zigging and zagging to catch them off guard. One warthog lost her footing as she turned and fell on the ground. Bulu barked crazily and did his mouthing act, pretending to bite her but not making contact. The warthog got up and started limping away. Steve shook his head at the workers. "One down, one to go!" The men were mes-

merized as they watched the game, eyes wide open, jaws slack. They had no idea that animals could *play*.

After tea break, raindrops began to ping on the metal roof as the men hammered away. They were used to working in the light rain. But during a downpour, they would seek shelter inside, beneath the completed section of roof. Hard rain would pour down onto the cement floor like a waterfall. Then within minutes, like someone had turned off a spigot, the rain would completely stop. And the men would go back to work. As Steve watched the drops dancing on the roof, he turned his face upward. He loved the feel of the cool rain on his face. *Wonderful Luangwa,* he thought. *No two moments ever the same.*

A voice suddenly called flatly from below. "What's wrong with Perky? She's limping." Steve looked down to see Anna under a big floppy canvas hat, an empty grass basket slung over her shoulder.

Steve leaned against a wood rail of the scaffolding. "She's a casualty from the great Bulu chase."

"I figured as much." She looked toward the hills. "I'd best get to the market before the next cloudburst." As Anna turned around, Bulu suddenly appeared next to her, his tail wagging.

"He spotted you carrying the basket," Steve laughed. "Never misses a chance for a ride. Thinks he's king of the road."

The Land Rover started to slide on the slick road and Anna switched to four-wheel drive. The rain pools along the way were like an obstacle course. Bulu stood in the passenger seat with his head out the window, eyes blinking against the stinging raindrops. Anna soon reached a narrow twenty-foot gully that completely crossed the road. *Ruff ruff.* Bulu was anxious to move. Anna knew he loved to see how the truck sprayed the water. She gunned the accelerator and cut through the

stream. The water parted into geysers, shooting ten feet up on each side of the vehicle. *Ruff ruff ruff ruff.*

About fifteen minutes later, Anna reached another gully, this one wider and deeper. She decided to stop and check it out before driving through. She took off her shoes and waded in as the mud sucked at her feet. It was about three feet deep in the middle. She returned to the truck. "Fasten your seat belt, Bulu." She revved the engine and plowed across the stream with a tremendous splash that washed over the hood like a wave. *RUFF RUFF RUFF RUFF.*

The gullies were getting deeper fast. Anna knew that if the storms increased, the tributaries would become torrents blocking the road. Above-average rainfall meant that the usually lazy Luangwa could turn into a turbulent white-water river. It could easily overflow its banks. Anna thought how fast she and Steve would be totally cut off. Their small aluminum boat—the size of a dinghy—would be far too dangerous to navigate when the river raged. They could be stranded for months, the water smothering the lowlands and encircling the house and wildlife center like a desert island. What would they do if they got sick or injured? Anna was determined to stock up on canned food, rice, flour, and other essentials to last for months. She continued to wrestle with the steering wheel on the slippery track, heading for the markets.

The sun briefly broke through the clouds over the construction site. Steve and the workers were sitting on the roof hammering down the last tin sheet. Two hours later, only one nail was left to complete the job.

Mabvuto smiled as he handed it to Steve, who raised his hammer and drove in the final nail. The men cheered and all shook hands.

With the roof finally up, Steve and Anna could begin work on the interior. In the morning, Steve would pay the workers their wages. In two days, the men would be folding up their tents and returning to their villages. They wanted to get home before the road washed out.

Steve was inside the center putting away his tools when he heard the truck. He stepped outside into the dusky light just as the vehicle stopped at the door. Anna waved as Bulu jumped out. Steve did a double take. The Land Rover had become a mountain, piled four feet high with crates and boxes. "I'm surprised you didn't sink!"

"We almost *did* in one gully." Anna swung out from the seat onto the ground and rubbed her arms. "Driving in mud is like steering a buffalo."

"The roof's done. We can store the nonperishables inside." Steve looked up at the clouds beginning to blanket the sun. "I'll get Mabvuto to bring lanterns and extra hands to help unload." Steve turned and headed toward the workers' tents. Bulu trotted after him, followed by his shadows, Pinky and Perky. As they crossed the grounds, Bulu halted and turned his head toward the river. He growled low. The warthogs stopped and turned their attention in the same direction. "What is it, Bulu?" Steve looked toward the river. Nothing was there. But Bulu and the warthogs continued to stare. They seemed to be listening to something far off, beyond human hearing. Steve shrugged and kept walking.

An hour later, Mabvuto and six other men had finished unloading the truck. Then, working like a bucket brigade, they relayed box after box into the center. The cinder block and stone building was divided into four spacious rooms, all still smelling strongly of fresh cement. Anna lit lanterns and placed them around for light.

For the rest of the evening, Steve and Anna sat on the floor opening boxes and organizing their contents. Pinky and Perky were stretched out close by, sound asleep. Bulu was sniffing about, inspecting every box, can, and container. "You never know, Bulu." Steve laughed. "You may get lucky and find the butter."

Anna leaned back against the wall. "I'm exhausted and famished." She looked at the seemingly endless stock of goods. "I'm going to the house to make tea and sandwiches." She groaned as she got up, massaging her cramped leg muscles. Picking up a large flashlight, she headed out the open doorway and into the night.

Bulu ran after her as lightning sparked across the

sky. Anna shone the powerful beam carefully across the ground. At night, she was always wary of the puff adder, a flat, thick, highly poisonous snake. Sluggish and camouflaged with mottled leaf patterns, it is easily stepped on. Electrified clouds flickered like hundreds of strobe lights all around her, momentarily lighting up the ground, house, and river. Then she heard Bulu growling behind her. Anna directed the light on him. He definitely had a bead on something. It gave her an uneasy feeling. She shone the flashlight all around and listened. Only the rushing of the river.

Wary, she decided to walk back to Steve. As she started to turn around, lightning ignited the riverbank for a moment in blue light. But like a snapshot, her eye had caught a large silhouette. She felt the hair rise on the nape of her neck. She pointed the beam at the shadow a hundred feet ahead. Large eyes reflected like headlights.

It was a lion. He faced her dead-on. Starting to hyperventilate, Anna was stunned when suddenly Bulu shot past her, barking madly, heading straight at the big cat. "BULU—STOP! *NO!*" Anna screamed. In a panic, she started to run after him, aiming the flashlight's beam at the lion's eyes. Bulu stopped a few yards away from the creature and stood his ground—barking and snarling like a rabid dog. The lion slowly turned, then loped back down the embankment. Bulu started to chase after him. *"NO—BULU—STOP!!!"* Bulu suddenly halted at the edge of the bank. Pumped with adrenaline and in shock, Anna ran up and grabbed him. "YOU STUPID, STUPID DOG!" she yelled, and gave him a good smack. "You could have *killed* us!" Bulu shrank into the ground. "You *never* learn. You *never* mind!" She burst into tears.

"Anna? Anna?" A spot of light wavered in the blackness as Steve came running up beside her. "What is it?! What is it?!"

"Stupid Bulu! A *lion*!" Anna choked out the words, barely making sense. "He tried to chase a lion!" She pointed to the bank. "Down there."

He aimed the flashlight at the river. The lion had gone. Steve put his arm around Anna, then shone the light on Bulu, who kept his head down. "So *that's* what you and the warthogs heard."

⟨◦⟩

Anna spread butter on bread as Steve opened a can of corned beef. Bulu lay on the floor, his head resting on his paws, eyes open, but diverted. The warthogs lay next to him. "He hasn't touched his food," said Steve.

"I don't even want to look at him," said Anna. "I keep thinking what could've happened. If the lion *hadn't* turned." She put down her knife and bread. "I've lost my appetite." She got up. "I'm taking a shower and going to bed."

Rain pounded on the roof as Anna lay awake. It was past midnight. She couldn't sleep. Something nagged at her as she listened to the hippos. She remembered how terrified Bulu was of the bull hippo. How he didn't try to confront it, but he didn't try to run from it either. Bulu understood the danger. Certainly he felt the same terror when he saw the lion. And then it dawned on her that perhaps Bulu wasn't chasing *after* the lion, but was instead chasing it *away*. That if Bulu hadn't chased the lion, she might have walked straight into it. That he had risked his life for her.

Tears came to her eyes. There was something she was dead certain about, something she had learned about him now. Bulu was a lot of things, but he was *never, ever* stupid.

"Only eighteen shopping days till Christmas," Steve said, pointing to the calendar pinned above the breakfast table. Anna laughed as she buttered her toast and looked out the window at the river. A troop of baboons was screaming and scrapping over some food on the bank. Steve nodded toward the baboons and grinned at Anna. "Reminds me of holiday shoppers." Anna's elbow shook, spilling her coffee. Bulu smelled butter and was nudging a few reminders. He put his head on her lap and gazed up, searching her face for any trace of anger from the night before. Anna looked down at his gentle eyes and intelligent face. "Sweet Bulu. Can you ever forgive me?" She put her hand on his head and he wagged his tail. Then she put extra butter on a piece of toast just for him.

BAM. The lightning startled Pinky and Perky. They trotted closer to Bulu, who was standing on top of the Chowo bridge. He was looking down at the wide, shallow body of water surging along the riverbed. Flash rains in the Nchendeni Hills were turning the dry Chowo into a stream again. A small tidal wave reached the viaduct and smacked against its cement foundation. Fascinated by the sudden swell of water that seemingly gushed out of nowhere, Bulu ran along the bridge to the bank as Pinky and Perky followed. Reaching the base, Bulu rushed into the gurgling water. It quickly turned into a game as Pinky and Perky splashed in after him.

Steve saw the trio race down the embankment as he headed to the workers' tents. The men were packing up to leave for their villages. Steve and Anna would then be completely left to their own devices. Steve singled out Mabvuto as the tents were being folded. "If you can learn to drive when you're back in Mfuwe, I can use you as our supply driver."

Mabvuto stood up excitedly from his tent bag.

Steve handed him an envelope. "This should pay for the school course. Give the letter to Hank. He'll direct you to the right person." Steve thought a moment about Mabvuto's fascination with tools and machinery. "And if you can learn something about repairing vehicles, I can give you a promotion."

"I can *do* this," Mabvuto said, shaking Steve's hand.

A few minutes later, Steve strode toward the Chowo

to see what Bulu and the warthogs were up to. He walked along the bridge and looked down the side of the ten-foot-high cement wall. Bulu was splashing about in the water with Pinky and Perky.

Steve sat on the viaduct and looked upriver. It was

still shallow, but he knew how quickly the streambed could fill deep. When the rains increased, the Chowo could turn into a gushing riptide within days. Watching Bulu, it occurred to him that the dog was just as crazy about water sports as the warthogs were. It made Steve uneasy. Bulu also liked to play in the Luangwa and often swam too far out. A few months ago, Steve and Anna learned of the tragedy that befell Bulu's mother. Hank told them how a dim-witted tourist had thrown a stick into the river for the dog to fetch. She splashed in to retrieve it, and before anyone knew what happened, a crocodile seized the dog and pulled her under.

But how could anyone keep Bulu away from the water?

Anna wrapped her present for Steve a few days before Christmas. Months earlier, she'd ordered a rare book on paleontology from England. As she folded an African print cloth tightly around the big book, she wondered what she could possibly make for Christmas dinner. A glance at the food pantry gave her an idea. Italian cuisine! She had both tomato paste and pasta. Little did she suspect that during the holiday meal, someone would bring the most bizarre Christmas present ever. Something that would steal her heart.

"Water rose higher than we thought last week," Steve said to Anna as they sat on the Chowo's bank, eating sandwiches during a rare break in the rain. The water was now running slightly over the bridge's narrow roadway. A few days earlier, Steve and Bulu had gone swimming in the deep pool created on the backwash of the viaduct. Like a couple of kids, the two had dived off the top to swim.

Nibbling her sandwich, Anna watched Bulu playing his mouthing games with Pinky and Perky. Steve got up and scanned the water. "I haven't seen any eyes staring back at us. I think it's clear of crocs." In a playful mood, he stripped off his shirt. "Bulu and I are going for a swim."

"Do you think it's safe?" Anna looked at the roll of the backwash wave against the viaduct wall. "The water's moving faster now. There could be an under-tow."

"We'll be fine," Steve reassured her. Bulu quickly got to his feet, whipping his tail back and forth in excite-ment. They walked across the shallow water flowing over the top of the bridge's roadway. When they reached the middle, Steve picked up Bulu and rocked him back and forth over the edge. *RUFF RUFF RUFF.* "Okay, big guy. *Heeere* we go!" Steve swung him over the edge and let fly. Bulu hit the water and went under. He had always surfaced fast on his dives, waiting for Steve to jump in after him. But this time, Bulu didn't come up. Without hesitation, Steve plunged into the water and disap-peared under the surface. He too didn't come up.

"Oh my God!" Anna jumped to her feet, her mind trying to comprehend the situation. "Come on, Steve . . ." A few more seconds went by. Her eyes des-perately searched the surface, but nothing broke. She knew this was not a game.

Steve had been sucked underwater by the undertow. In the roiling turbulence, he opened his eyes to look for Bulu. But he could see nothing in the murky water. He felt about . . . and was shocked to *feel* Bulu right beside him! He grabbed him, then kicked his legs as fast as he could toward the surface.

Anna saw Bulu suddenly appear above the water about twenty feet away from the bridge. Steve was holding him up. But they were being dragged closer and closer to the roiling water near the bridge. She screamed when she watched Steve and Bulu sucked under again.

Caught in the undertow, Steve kept an astounding presence of mind, holding on to Bulu tightly in his right arm. Letting go of him this time, he knew, would mean losing Bulu forever. Steve put his full strength into his left arm and his legs, straining every muscle to reach the surface.

Anna was just about to jump in after them when Bulu suddenly resurfaced again, held aloft by a hand. Steve's head appeared, then his shoulders. With both hands, he forcefully pushed the dog toward shallow water, away from the undertow. A moment later, Bulu reached the bank and climbed it. But Steve's efforts had exhausted him. To Anna's horror, he was pulled back to the center and sucked under again. He surfaced briefly, gulping for air, then disappeared below the surface. Anna screamed, a chilling primeval sound. She believed Steve had now drowned.

Underwater, desperately holding his breath, Steve

was pulled up against the cement wall like a magnet. His lungs felt like they were imploding. Knowing this time he would surely drown, he made one last fateful decision. He was not going to swim upward to the surface. He was going to try to swim underwater, straight away from the bridge and the vortex of water smashing against it. Gathering all his remaining strength, he planted his feet against the wall, bent his knees like a spring, and pushed hard. As though torpedoing himself away from the vortex, he broke loose of the undertow's grip. Then, with his arms moving in powerful, adrenaline-charged strokes, he finally reached the surface and gulped for air. His feet touched a submerged log. It was just high enough so that he could stand on it and keep his head above the water.

Anna stood on the bank in a dream state. After a few moments, Steve caught his breath. Regaining some strength, he swam toward the shore, his arms sweeping the water in slow, strong strokes. Anna raced down to the water. When Steve reached the bank, she clasped his arm and helped him up. He lay on his back, lungs heaving, his body pale and shivering. Anna slumped to the ground beside him. Then she started yelling at him. "I warned you about the undertow! You wouldn't listen!" Her hands shot to her face. "I thought you had drowned!" She started to sob uncontrollably. "I thought . . . that . . . you were *dead*." She got to her feet and ran back to the house.

For the next few days, Anna could barely speak to Steve. She was still upset that his careless games had nearly ended in tragedy. Steve moved about the house a bit sheepishly. Even Bulu was a bit subdued as he lay on the floor.

Early Christmas Eve morning, Anna began making preparations for the holiday dinner. While Steve worked at the wildlife center making display shelves, Anna worked in the house. She set the table with a bright red and green tablecloth. Their Christmas tree was a potted three-foot-high mahogany sapling that she'd later plant outside. She found colorful scraps of African print cloths, shaped them into bows, and tied them onto the branches. Placing candles around the room, she glanced at the present she'd wrapped for Steve. She thought how terrifyingly close she'd come to losing him. She reflected that *this* Christmas must certainly be blessed.

The clouds smothered the dusky light at the windows as Anna lit the candles. The room was soon glimmering with holiday spirit. Steve stood by the table turning the corkscrew on a bottle of South African wine. Bulu was at his feet. The warthogs were lying in the cool shower stall. Spaghetti sauce gurgled on the stove, sending an aroma of garlic and oregano throughout the room. The cork popped and Steve poured red wine into goblets. Anna took her seat. Steve sat down and raised his glass for a toast. "To a romantic evening. And a very merry Christmas." They clicked their glasses. Just as Anna got up to get the pasta from the stove, something rumbled in the distance. This time it wasn't thunder, but a truck engine grinding up the drive. "*Who* could be coming here on Christmas Eve?" Anna asked, raising her eyebrows.

Steve got up and grabbed a flashlight. "I don't think it's going to be Santa."

Opening the door, he shaded his eyes against the headlight beams in the dark. When the vehicle pulled up alongside the house, he could just make out ZAWA printed on the mud-splattered doors. "Someone from the Zambia Wildlife Authority," Steve called back to Anna. "Wonder what's up to come so late?"

The truck's door opened. A heavyset Zambian man wearing a green ZAWA uniform and black boots stepped out. He tipped his green beret. "Mister Steve?" Steve shook his hand just as Anna and Bulu appeared at the door. "Miss Anna?" The man bowed slightly and handed Steve a letter. "I am Officer Njovu. I been instructed to deliver you something from headquarters."

Steve looked down the mud-soaked driveway. "How did you ever make it through the gullies?"

"When I get stuck, he pushes." Njovu chuckled, acknowledging the young ranger getting out of the truck. "I born in Luangwa. This not now bad rain." Njovu then opened the rear door. He lifted out a wooden crate covered with a blanket and handed it to Steve. Bulu immediately picked up a scent. He started sniffing the air and jumping up to see inside.

"You can look. He no harm you," Njovu said to Steve. In the glow of the headlights, Steve slowly began to pull back the blanket. Through the thin chicken wire mesh, something the size of a puppy was staring back at him. It had black saucer eyes, huge hairless ears, and a head that seemed too big for its body. And a tail, like a snake, curled around its long legs.

Anna took the flashlight and shone it inside the crate. "Oh, Steve!" She put her hand to her heart. "A baby vervet." She carefully opened the wire door. "He's beautiful."

"Beautiful?" Steve looked askance. "He looks like an alien from outer space!"

Anna reached inside the crate and picked him up. The baby immediately grasped his little fingers tight onto her blouse. "He can't be more than a couple of weeks old. He's adorable." Bulu started to jump even higher to get a better look.

Steve opened the letter and held up the flashlight to read it. His jaw went slack. "Oh, swell—we're supposed to raise it." He grimaced at Anna and handed her the letter. "We'll see how *adorable* a monkey can be living in a one-room house with two people, one dog, and two warthogs!"

Anna ignored him and smiled at Officer Njovu. "Won't you and the ranger kindly join us for Christmas dinner?"

Sitting at the candlelit table, Steve asked Njovu why ZAWA had sent them a monkey. The vervet clung to Anna's neck as she served spaghetti.

"No, *two* monkeys, Mister Steve," Njovu corrected him.

Steve and Anna glanced at each other in bewilderment.

"What do you mean . . . *two*?" Steve pointed at the vervet. "There is only one monkey."

"Yes." Njovu nodded. "Only one *here*."

"But where's the *other* monkey?" Anna asked.

"He at ZAWA headquarters. We found him near there," said Njovu. "Your monkey. We find abandon near village. We bring other monkey here soon."

"*Soon?*" Steve asked, noticing the mischievous smile on the officer's face. "Why didn't you bring him with *this* monkey?"

"*Other* monkey. He need to rehydrate first," Njovu explained. "And *other* monkey scream all the time. *Scare* this monkey bad." He shot a sly grin at the ranger across the table.

"Yes, he scream, scream, *screeeam*!" The ranger underscored the point. "*Eeeeee! Eeeeee!* Make people *craaazy*." He chuckled as he buttered his bread. Then his elbow started shaking. He looked down in shock. Bulu was staring up at him, demanding his share of the butter.

"The dog. He *live* in house?" the ranger asked.

Njovu wasn't the only one now grinning impishly. "Yes," Steve said. "Bulu shares the house with a couple of unusual friends." He got up and walked over to the shower stall. "Would you like to meet them?"

Njovu and the ranger looked cautiously toward the shower's screen. Steve clapped. Out came the warthogs. Njovu and the ranger did a double take.

"Meet Pinky and Perky," Anna announced as they trotted into the room. The warthogs quickly lay down on their sides and Steve started tickling their bellies. Njovu and the ranger looked at each other and burst into laughter. "ZAWA say you know how to raise warthogs. But not as friends!" Njovu shook his head in amazement. "Then maybe you have no problem raising monkeys."

Anna lifted her wineglass for a toast. "Merry Christmas, gentlemen. Peace on earth and goodwill toward . . . *warthogs.*"

Njovu took a sip of wine and turned serious for a moment. "Mister Steve. Miss Anna. Please know ZAWA will not permit you keep wild animals for long. Only till they learn to live in wild." He sat back in his chair observing Steve with the warthogs and Anna with the vervet. "Try not become friends with them too much. Otherwise, setting them free could break heart."

11

Plink. A drop of water fell on Steve's face. He woke and looked up to see another drop about to fall through the mosquito net. The pillow was damp. "Great, just what I need on New Year's Day. A leak in a thatch haystack." He leaned forward on one elbow and saw Anna seated at the breakfast table, feeding the monkey. Then he got up, slipped on his shirt and shorts, and headed for the coffeepot.

"I don't think raising another vervet is going to be a problem," Anna said, holding a medicine dropper to the baby's lips. "They're helpless orphans and so sweet." The monkey reached out for a fork on the table. He turned it over and over to examine it. Then he did the same thing with the spoon and knife. "Flint! Of course."

"What?" Steve asked as he poured coffee.

"His name. We'll call him Flint," she laughed. "He reminds me of you. The way you scrutinize every fossil or piece of flint you find."

Steve raised an eyebrow at Anna. Then something

caught his attention at the open door. "*Oh no!* Look out!"

A "brown" dog and two seemingly chocolate-covered warthogs bounded through the doorway. Bulu immediately began to shake, splattering Steve, Anna, and the monkey with mud. Pinky and Perky trotted up to Steve. It was time for their morning grooming and massage. They instantly lay down on their sides. Steve scratched their ears and muddy, bloated bellies. He pulled clumps of mud from their wiry hair, making it stand up like on a punky porcupine.

Flint stretched his head forward, eyes popping, fascinated by the animal antics. Bulu trotted over and licked the monkey's ears. Flint's little fingers reached out and examined Bulu's ears . . . then pulled *hard*. "Monkey see, monkey do, Bulu," Anna laughed.

Steve got out an old brush and groomed Pinky's and Perky's coarse, wrinkled hides. Their eyes rolled heavenward in ecstasy. "Ah, my beauties. Come April, warthog gentlemen will be knocking at your burrow."

"Which means you'd better get started building one," said Anna. "They'll be having babies of their own soon."

By the end of the week, the rains had gotten heavier. Storms rumbled like kettledrums, and bloated black clouds sagged over the hills. Torrents of water let loose into the gullies and flowed continuously into the Luangwa.

Steve struggled to push a wheelbarrow loaded with cinder blocks through the muddy ground. He set it down beside the half-finished cement burrow, located a hundred feet from the house. The seven-by-seven-foot warthog den would stand four feet high when finished.

The morning sun barely penetrated the mist resting

above the river. Steve was unloading the blocks when Anna walked up with Bulu beside her. Flint was on her shoulder, hands clinging to her neck. "I'm worried about the river," Anna said. "It's rising much faster than we anticipated."

"I know. If it begins to overflow the banks, we'll need to evacuate to the center."

Anna raised her eyebrows. "And if the center floods?"

Steve grinned and reached over to tickle the monkey. "We'll join Flint in the trees."

Bulu trotted out of the center toward the truck turning onto the driveway. Steve and Anna followed as the ZAWA vehicle pulled alongside. "Mister Steve." Njovu saluted. "I bring you something again."

"Let me guess, Njovu." Steve forced a half smile. "The *other* monkey?"

Njovu beamed as he got out. He reached across the seat, picked up a blanket-covered crate, and handed it to Steve. Anna stepped closer to put her face near the blanket. Flint, clinging to her neck, sensed something and stretched his neck forward. Gingerly, Steve pulled back the blanket. A little face showed through the wire mesh. Flint freaked. *Eeeeee eeeeee eeeeeee.* He recognized the other monkey. Inside the box, the second baby vervet's eyes shot open. He freaked too. EEEEEEEE EEEEEEEE EEEEEEEE. This set Bulu off. He started barking and jumping up and down to try to look into the crate. *EEEEEEEEEEEEEEEE.*

Steve cringed. "*This* monkey shrieks louder than the biker gangs in a Mad Max movie. Does he ever stop screaming?"

"Only when he sleep," said Njovu. He looked up at the sky. "Bad rains come soon." He paused and chuckled at Steve. "*Two* monkeys and *two* warthogs now live *in house* with you during rains. Very nice, yes?"

"Yes, Njovu. Very nice and cozy. Thanks."

Njovu stepped up into the truck, waved, and drove off.

Steve put the blanket over the crate and the monkey hushed momentarily. He turned to Anna. "Looks like we've got our hands full."

Inside the house, Steve gently placed the crate down on the floor. Pinky and Perky were lying beside the shower stall. Steve slowly removed the blanket and unlatched the crate's door. Bulu sat down on his haunches a few feet away and stared. "Okay, Mad Max," Steve said softly. "Take a look at your new home."

A moment later, the crate door creaked open. The monkey's little head peeked out. As his huge eyes adjusted to the light, he peered around at his new surroundings. Slowly, he ventured out of his box and crept across the floor into the middle of the room. Pinky and Perky got up to investigate. *EEEEEEEEEE.* Max had spotted the warthogs. In a split second, he zipped across the room, squeezed behind the bookcase, and got stuck. His face registered pure terror as the warthogs moved closer. With no alternative, he let out a supersonic shriek. *EEEEEEEEEEEEEEEE.* Then Flint began to scream, digging his fingers into Anna's neck. *Eeeeeeeeeeeeeeeee.*

Anna clasped her hands over her ears as Steve rushed over to the bookcase. "Out! Out!" He shooed the warthogs to the door.

"Something traumatic certainly happened to Max's family for him to be abandoned," Anna said. "He's still so distressed!"

"Maybe a leopard killed his mother?" Steve shrugged.

Bulu sat strangely quiet, intently watching. Then he stood up and walked over to the freaked-out vervet. When he got within two feet, Bulu sat down and stared. Moments later, Max stopped shrieking and focused on the dog. Perhaps thinking the screams had been a distress call, Bulu walked right up to Max and laid his muzzle on the monkey's neck. Then, just as he had done with Pinky, Perky, and Flint, Bulu snuffled and licked the now-quiet Max.

Steve and Anna shook their heads, marveling at Bulu's understanding of the critical situation. Putting his arm around Anna, Steve said, "I remember reading an amazing article about a collie dog that jumped off a cliff to save his master. The man had slipped and fallen sixty feet into a shallow stream. He was knocked unconscious, with his face underwater. The dog instantly sized up the situation, leapt into the gorge, and broke both hips! But he managed to *crawl* to his master and kept the man's head above water till help arrived."

Anna sat at the breakfast table holding Flint in the crook of her arm. Bulu was at Steve's feet waiting for his toast. Watching Flint being fed, Max edged out of his cage and crept toward the table. He sat down beside Bulu and put his little hands around one of the dog's front legs. Bulu licked him on the ears. Gradually gathering his courage, Max climbed onto the chair beside Anna. When Flint dozed off, Anna placed him in his box bed on the table. As though it were the most natural thing to do, Max then climbed onto Anna's lap. He lay back and allowed her to put the medicine dropper to his lips. He guzzled the milk.

Steve smiled at the contented domestic scene. Then he pointed up at the thatched roof. Drops of water dripped continuously into a bucket. "Repair day. I'd better get on it before it gets worse."

Standing on a ladder against the house, Steve inspected the roof and found the leak. He hoped to fix it before the next rain. As he began to lay new thatch over the hole, something caught his eye. It was Bulu trotting off into the woods. Steve noticed how Bulu was becoming bolder, even fiercely territorial with bigger animals that stepped on the property. Weeks before, he had chased away a large kudu antelope that had the cheek to step too close to the center.

Moments later, Steve had started to tie down the thatch when he heard a series of *thump thump thumps* on the soggy ground below. He looked down just in time to see a puku buck run past like a racehorse toward the river. It leapt from the bank in a graceful arc and hit the water with a splash. Aware that nearby crocodiles might hear the smack on the water, Steve was alarmed to see the puku heading toward midstream. Then, to his horror, Steve saw another splash at the river's edge. It was Bulu! He seemed to appear from nowhere and was now swimming fast after the puku. "BULU—NO! *BULU!*" Steve shouted as he scrambled down the ladder and ran to the riverbank. His yells brought Anna racing out the door. Rounding the house, she saw the puku swimming midriver followed by a small white and brown head barely visible above the surface. *"BULU!"* she screamed, running up to Steve. The puku reached the far bank, climbed up, and ran into the trees. Steve and Anna watched helplessly as Bulu fought the current, swimming toward the far embankment. As he scrambled up, the mud gave way and he fell back into the river. Finally getting his footing, he made another attempt and struggled to the top. He stood still a moment looking around as though coming to his senses. Seeming to panic, he ran to the left and then to the right trying to find a safe way back. But there was no safe way across the swollen river.

"What can we do?" Anna was frantic, clinging to Steve's arm.

"I'm going for the boat!" he shouted, turning on his heel and racing for the storeroom at the center. But before he got fifty yards away, he heard Anna scream. He rushed back and saw Bulu was in the water again, his neck stretched forward, trying to keep his head above the current. Steve's eyes scanned the water's surface and he thought of the gruesome fate of Bulu's mother. Anna was frozen, her hands covering her mouth in terror. But there

was nothing they could do except watch in dread as Bulu swam back. For what seemed like an eternity, he swam on and on, slowly being pulled downstream. At one point, the force of the river spun him completely around. As though giving it his last effort, he paddled harder, letting the current take him into calmer water nearer the bank. Steve ran downstream and waded into the shallows. He held out his hands as Bulu swam toward him. In one quick move he grabbed the dog around the middle and hauled him out of the water. Bulu was limp from exhaustion. Steve laid him on the bank. Anna ran up beside them. Tears streaming down her face, she put her hand on Bulu's fast-beating heart. Steve's and Anna's eyes met. No words were needed. They knew that by some grace Bulu had been spared.

The baboon was kept chained to a tree behind the old Chipata gas station at the Zambia-Malawi border post. When kids passed by, they threw pebbles at the creature until it ran the length of its chain. They thought it funny when the steel collar yanked its neck. The scene would be repeated over and over throughout the day.

Then one rainy afternoon, Mitch was returning from a safari in Malawi and stopped for fuel at the Chipata station. While a man filled the Land Rover's tank, Mitch walked to the little tea kiosk behind the station. Pulling his canvas hat over his face against the drizzle, he stepped among the rubble of old tires and wheels. He would have missed the tiny figure huddled under the tree if it were not for the whimpering. Thinking the sound came from a child, Mitch turned his head and pushed his hat back. He was astonished to see a small, miserable baboon staring at him.

The baboon was male, about a year old. He had

brown matted hair and was emaciated. His left eye was slightly smaller and off center from the right eye. His neck was a mass of bleeding sores, his chest encrusted with dried blood. "Good afternoon, old boy." Mitch spoke softly as he glanced around at the trash surrounding the tree. "Hardly a place for a dignified young gentleman, now is it?" The baboon lowered his doglike face and fiddled with his hands as though embarrassed by his predicament. "We must do something about this." Mitch looked toward the small house behind the back of the gas station. "I shall have a word or two with your owner."

Mitch pulled the Land Rover up to the cement building of ZAWA headquarters and turned off the engine. "Mister Mitch, what bring you here?" Njovu asked, stepping off the porch.

"A baboon." Mitch climbed out and walked to the back of the truck to swing open the rear door.

Njovu followed him and saw the baboon sitting on a blanket with a white bandage around his neck. "A snare do this?"

"No. A collar. The manager of a gas station had him chained up as a 'freak' attraction. He was captured as a baby after someone shot the mother. I paid to buy his freedom."

"Baboon not try to bite you?" Njovu looked incredulous.

"No. The little chap's surprisingly gentle. He likes being talked to softly. I won his trust. Then I cleaned his wounds. Do you know anyone who could care for him? At least until a wild troop might accept him?"

"No, I do not know—" Njovu interrupted himself. "Wait! I know someone who could. Mister Steve and Miss Anna. They have two monkeys now. And two warthogs."

Mitch raised his eyebrows. "I knew about the warthogs. But they now have monkeys?"

"Yes. Vervets. I can take this baboon to them."

"But the road will be impassable now. There's no way to get the baboon to their place."

Njovu smiled triumphantly. "We have *boat*," he crowed gleefully as he folded his arms and leaned against the Land Rover. "I think Mister Steve be *very* happy. Now he can have baboon live inside house too."

Rain tapped on the roof of the cement warthog den. Steve was hammering on the last piece of tin sheeting to finish the structure. As he reached down for another box of nails, he saw the tail end of a snake slip behind some bushes thirty feet away. It happened so fast that he could not immediately identify the species. But he believed it was a cobra by its thickness and dark gray skin. He looked over to the house and saw Bulu with the warthogs. Bulu had not spotted the snake. But Steve was still concerned. Snakes sometimes take up residence inside buildings during the rains. As the downpour increased, he decided to stop work. Starting to walk back to the house, he heard the hum of a motor in the distance. The door of the house opened and Anna stepped out. She had heard it too. Bulu ran toward the river, followed by the warthogs.

Standing on the riverbank in their slickers, Steve and Anna waited for the boat. Bulu stood beside them, his eyes focused on the bend of the river. Within moments, a twenty-foot-long powerboat droned into view, its wake disturbing the grumbling hippos. It was the ZAWA launch. In the front seat was Njovu steering. In the middle sat three rangers in waterproof fatigues and hats. In the backseat sat a figure covered in a plastic tarp.

As the launch moved close to the bank, one of the rangers threw a rope to Steve, who tied it to a log. Steve then recognized the man steering the boat. "Njovu!" he shouted over the engine noise. "Don't tell us you brought us another monkey."

Njovu laughed, tipping his beret. "No. But your friend has."

The man in the back quickly lifted the tarp and grinned.

"A *baboon*!" Anna blurted out.

"I've been called worse." Mitch laughed as he looked down at the baboon clinging tightly to his waist. "Njovu's kindly offered you this baboon for safekeeping."

"*Another* monkey?" Steve groaned.

"Oh, he's been hurt," Anna said, noticing the bandage around the baboon's neck. "What happened?"

"He'd been chained up at a gas station at Chipata. I rescued him," Mitch said, stepping out of the boat.

"I'll make tea and lunch for everyone," Anna offered.

"We can't stay, I'm afraid," Mitch apologized. "Njovu has to take me straight back to headquarters. They're doing patrols upriver this afternoon." As Mitch petted the baboon, Bulu slowly walked forward to sniff. The baboon gazed quietly at the dog. Mitch chuckled as the warthogs walked up to investigate too. "Bulu. I see you're still the foster dad. Think you can handle a baboon?"

"We almost lost Bulu a couple of weeks ago," Steve said. "Chased a puku across the river."

Mitch looked to the water and shook his head. "Mister Bulu. Now don't be gambling all nine of your lives at once."

"Sorry, but we must go now, Mister Mitch," Njovu said.

With some reluctance, Mitch gently pulled the baboon's arms free from his waist. The baboon tried to hold on but didn't make a sound. Steve stepped forward and gently picked him up. The baboon wrapped his arms around Steve's chest.

"Never underestimate his intelligence," Mitch said. "There's a true story about a pet baboon in South Africa, back in the 1880s, that knew how to switch railway tracks. In response to a whistle signal, the baboon pulled the correct lever. He never got it wrong! He learned how to do it after his human 'master' lost both legs in an accident." Mitch shook his head and thought a moment. He reached out his hand and caught the outstretched fingers of the baboon. "I believe his name was Jack."

Anna walked forward and gave Mitch a hug and

kiss. He smiled as a ranger handed over two big burlap bags of food to Anna. "He loves bananas and peanuts." Then Mitch turned and stepped into the launch. Njovu revved the engine, and they were off.

As the boat disappeared around the bend, the baboon watched intently. Steve looked down at him and smiled. "Don't worry, we'll take good care of you . . . Jack."

Steve carried Jack into the house as Bulu followed closely behind. Flint, lying in his cage, suddenly let out a screech when he saw the baboon. The noise woke Max in his cage. When he spotted the baboon, his eyes practically shot out of their sockets. *EEEEEEEEEEEEEEEEE.* He released an eardrum-shattering scream and flattened himself against the back of his cage.

"It's okay, guys, it's okay." Steve tried to calm them. "Meet gentle Jack." Bulu trotted over to peer into Max's cage and lay down in front of it. His presence calmed Max and he stopped screaming.

"I don't think Flint and Max have ever seen a baboon before," Anna said, opening the burlap bags.

"Jack probably never saw a Mad Max before," Steve laughed. "Or a Bulu."

Anna pulled bananas and peanuts from the bags and put them on the floor. Jack whimpered excitedly as Steve put him down. Instantly, the baboon grabbed a banana and peeled and devoured it. Then he started on the peanuts, the shells piling up fast. Bulu walked over, sat down, and watched Jack.

Perhaps because Bulu was so placid in the presence of the baboon, Flint came out of his cage and moved closer to the strange monkey. It was some time before Max got up his courage, but eventually he too crept out

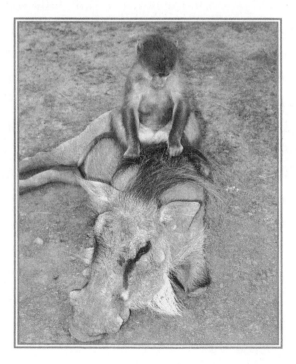

of his cage. Steve winked at Anna. Max was ever so slowly scooting across the floor. He stopped when he got close to Bulu and Flint. Then all three sat together silently, fixated on every movement of the serene, most entertaining baboon. It looked like the trio had accepted the new kid on the block.

Then one morning, Jack began to do something mysterious. Steve and Anna were eating breakfast when they noticed tiny piles of soggy mashed peanuts and bananas under the table. At first it worried them. Was the baboon ill? The mystery was solved one day when they noticed Max crawling under the table. Steve and Anna peeked to discover Jack was chewing up his food, then taking mashed bits from his mouth and putting them on the floor for Max to eat. It appeared that the baboon—once a victim of heartless abuse—*understood* that the nervous little vervet needed special care.

Day after day, the rains continued to fill the Luangwa. Each morning, Steve and Anna walked to the river to see how much it had risen during the night. The water level was now, alarmingly, only a few feet from the lip of the embankment.

Despite the increasingly heavy downpours, Bulu's

enthusiasm for his bush jaunts never dampened. One morning as he trotted out with Pinky and Perky, Flint and Max started to follow. But when the vervets reached the doorway, they were too timid to go farther. They sat down and watched the dog and warthogs head for the woodlands.

Inside the house, the baboon followed Steve everywhere, including the shower. "Oh no." Steve sighed as he grabbed the shampoo. "Can't I have one second of peace and privacy?" As he lathered up, Jack sat down and watched despite the splashing of water and soap. Steve heard Anna giggle from the breakfast table. "I think you've become Jack's big brother," she said. "You're his hero."

"A role model for a baboon? Great." Steve squinted through soapsuds at Jack.

"Why not?" Anna laughed. "I married one, didn't I?"

⟐

A while later, Bulu trotted in the door just as Steve was walking out to the Land Rover. "You're just in time to help haul rations from the storeroom," Steve said as he bent over to pet him. Bulu looked startled. The baboon clung to Steve's back, his long arms wrapped around

Steve's neck. "That is, if I can get this monkey off my back." He gently took Jack's hands to release his grip and then held him in one arm. Steve climbed in the truck and set the baboon on the seat beside the window. *Grrrrrr.* Bulu growled and gave a sharp bark. "Uh-oh, Jack." Steve chuckled. "This could turn ugly. You're in Master Bulu's seat!" Steve put Jack on his lap. Then Bulu hopped in and took his rightful place beside the window.

When Steve pulled up beside the center's entryway, thunderclouds ripped open like a burst water tank, rain rushing down on the truck's roof. In what seemed like seconds, all visibility was obliterated. "Well, Bulu," Steve said, squinting into the storm. "It's no longer a question of *if* the Luangwa and Chowo will flood. It's now a matter of *when.*"

13

Tossed and turned by the surge of white water, the tree slammed into the Chowo bridge like a torpedo, cracking open a four-foot-wide hole in the concrete. Standing on the embankment, Steve and Anna were astonished by the power of the water. Jack was on Steve's back, clinging tightly, bug-eyed in alarm. Bulu sat on his haunches, mesmerized by logs spinning on the foaming surface like matchsticks. Ever since his experience of chasing the puku across the river, Bulu kept a safe distance from fast water. Roaring brown waves pulverized the banks, exposing tree roots and wrenching out bushes. The current looked like it was shooting out of a giant fire hose.

"The bridge can't take much more punishment," Steve said, watching debris crash into the viaduct. "If it goes, we're completely cut off."

It was now nearing the end of January. From year to year it was impossible to predict the intensity and duration of the rainy season, from November to March.

The previous year, the water had almost overflowed the banks.

As Steve and Anna watched the churning Chowo, they could only guess what the rain gods had in store this year. By the look of things, the house was in real danger of flooding.

Later in the morning, the two trudged through the mud to the center to continue working on wildlife exhibits. The center was slated to open in April, but the continual heavy downpours could delay it indefinitely.

That night back at the house, Steve and Anna sat reading at the table as lightning lit up the sky. *Eeeeeeee eeeeeeeee eeeeeeeee.* Max made a mad dash from the table to his sleeping cage and crawled in. Bulu moved over to the cage and sat down in front of it until Max stopped screaming. Then Jack and Flint walked over to sit beside Bulu. It seemed like they were all watching over Max.

"Do you think he'll ever get over his jitters?" Anna asked.

"I don't know. If he's afraid of everything beyond our door," Steve said, watching the lightning through the windows, "how can he ever return to the wild?"

Anna shrugged, stood up, and yawned. She picked up her book and went to lie down on the bed. As soon as she started to read again, she drifted off to sleep. Moments later, Steve started to nod off and went to bed too.

Long after midnight, the thunder finally subsided. The silence was punctuated by the murmur of insects. Bulu, lying by Max's cage, suddenly put his head up. *Squish squish squish squish.* A faint sound of footsteps. Bulu got to his feet, jumped up onto a chair, and looked out the window into the blackness. He could see nothing through the drizzle. *Squish squish squish squish.*

Bulu started a low growl as the footfalls moved closer to the house. He jumped down and ran over to the reed wall. *Ruff ruff ruff ruff.*

Steve and Anna woke with a start. "What is it?" Steve reached for the flashlight beside the bed.

Jack, Flint, and Max had awakened. They watched Bulu sniffing and growling along the wall.

Anna leaned forward and listened. "Do you hear that?"

"Yes. Something big is out there." Steve got to his feet.

Anna got out of bed. "I'll hold on to Bulu."

Steve followed the flashlight beam across the room. Reaching the doorway, he put his hand on the latch and quietly pulled down on it. As the door creaked open, he listened for the footfalls. Nothing. Only the dripping of water from the roof into puddles. He aimed his flashlight outside into the mist. What he saw confounded him. He was staring at what appeared to be two mottled tree trunks—with knees! Then he smiled and turned back into the house. "Shhh. You've got to see this."

Anna picked up Bulu and walked over to stand beside Steve at the doorway. He aimed a beam of light at the tree trunks, which now *moved.* Anna let out a gasp. Bulu let out a bark. Great long legs swung forward like giant pendulums, plopping down platter-sized hooves into the muck. *Squish squish squish squish.* Steve raised the flashlight higher to reveal the full magnificence of the eighteen-foot visitor, a bull giraffe. It stopped a moment in freeze-frame and stared downward into the shaft of light. Perhaps deciding whether to stand its ground or flee, the giraffe stomped one foot. Bulu began his long, low growl.

Anna started to chuckle. "Shhh," she whispered. "He's much bigger than you." The giraffe slowly turned and paced toward the woodlands. His body undulated in the rhythm of his measured footsteps, like a giant rocking horse. When Bulu narrowed his eyes in defiance, Anna laughed out loud. "Oh, Bulu." She put her cheek next to his face. "Our great protector from giants." The giraffe faded into the mist. "Even gentle ones."

Steve crawled back into bed as Anna stretched out on the old couch to read. But soon her eyelids became heavy, and she turned down the lantern. Flashes of light and thunder continued to disturb the monkeys.

A few minutes later, Steve was awakened when he heard giggling. Annoyed, he got up to see what was so funny. He switched on the flashlight and walked over to Anna. He broke into a big grin. There on the couch, all cuddled together on top of Anna, were Jack, Flint, and

even shy Max. They were entangling their arms together, wriggling to share the small space. Bulu was trying to jump on board too. Steve reached down to pet him. "It looks like, at long last, we've become one big happy family." He looked over at the shower stall, where the warthogs were sleeping. "Maybe a bit strange . . . but by golly, Bulu, we're a family."

Early one morning, Steve came tearing into the house. *"The bridge collapsed!"* Anna, washing dishes at the sink, looked at him in disbelief. "Grab your slicker! February's roared in like a lion." Steve raced back out the door. Bulu perked up from his food bowl and quickly trotted after him. As Anna stepped out of the house, she saw them disappear into the blinding rain. Only their footprints in the mud guided her toward the Chowo.

A few minutes later, she reached the embankment where Steve and Bulu stood. Driving rain pelted the hood of her slicker like hail. Wiping water from her face, she tried to focus. When she spotted the black outline of the viaduct, it took a moment to register. The center of the bridge was gone . . . like dynamite had blasted it away. White water gushed and roared through the gap. Anna shook her head. She tried to be heard above the wind, which was tearing the words from her mouth. "Steve! I don't think we'll be going anywhere for a while!"

He squinted up into the storm and shouted back, "It's going to get worse before it gets better!"

By mid-February, the Luangwa had risen to the lip of the embankment. Bright sunny breaks in the weather gave false hope that the water would recede. But rain over the escarpment and the hills continuously plunged down to swell the gullies.

One morning, after a particularly violent thunderstorm, Steve opened the door to let out Pinky and Perky. Bulu walked out too and suddenly stopped in his tracks, staring toward the river. Wondering what caught Bulu's attention, Steve stepped outside. He was jolted to see the river slopping over the bank! Like a miniature tsunami, a half-foot wave of floodwater was steadily flowing toward the house. He hurried back inside and shook Anna awake. "The river's spilling over and heading this

way! Gather the animals two by two. I'm going for the ark." He grabbed the Land Rover keys and raced out. Just as he opened the truck door, Bulu appeared and hopped up into the seat.

At the center, Steve ran into the storeroom for the

dinghy. He looked at the small five-horsepower outboard engine but decided the water was not deep
enough for it. He then picked up an eight-foot punting
pole. He could use it to propel the small boat through
the shallow water. He dragged the dinghy outside to the
truck. Looking toward the house, he was shocked to see
the water was already beginning to encircle the foundation. "There's no time to lose now, Bulu," Steve said,
climbing into the seat. Because the house rested several
yards below the level of the center, it would be the first
to flood.

Back at the house, Steve off-loaded the boat from
the truck. Inside, Anna was rushing about stashing perishable food into boxes. Then she started packing their
precious books. Sitting on the dining table, Jack, Flint,
and Max watched the flurry of activity. Steve grabbed
the rifles from the wall racks and put them in their steel
containers. He snatched up the cameras, lenses, and
binoculars. When he looked out the window toward the
river, he saw that the floor of the gazebo was already
under several inches of water.

For the rest of the morning, Steve feverishly made
trips back and forth in the Land Rover between the
house and the center. He transported the bed, couch,
tables, chairs, camping equipment, and boxes of books.

Although the stove and refrigerator had to be left behind, he disconnected the propane tanks. They could be used with the portable camp stove at the center.

The rising water was fast turning the sandy ground to mush. Despite the Land Rover's four-wheel drive, it began to lose its grip and the tires were wildly spitting out muck. On each trip, the truck sank deeper and deeper. Before it got permanently stuck, Steve decided to park it on higher ground at the center. He now needed to rely solely on the boat to haul everything. He tied a rope to the prow and towed it behind him. Hour after hour, he transported goods back and forth. Bulu followed him on every trip, having to swim in places.

By noon, the water had reached a two-foot depth inside the house. Steve had tied the dinghy to a wall post beside the door for loading. He and Anna were rushing about the room gathering canned goods from shelves. Jack, Flint, and Max had perched themselves on top of the bookcase, alarmed by the rising water. Steve started lifting more boxes into the boat. By the time he'd loaded it, the water's depth had reached three feet. He grabbed his punting pole and stepped into the dinghy. Bulu couldn't get a leg up into it because the water was now over his head. Steve reached over and pulled him in. Bulu quickly took the seat at the prow of the boat. "Hate

to tell you, Captain Bulu," Steve laughed, "but the captain always goes down with his ship."

Steve continued to go back and forth in the dinghy hauling clothes, blankets, medical supplies, lanterns, and household utensils. The center's largest room was now crowded with boxes. While there was still some daylight, he set up the bed. Then he hung the large mosquito net over it. "There's only one thing left to do, Captain," Steve said to Bulu as they walked to the boat. "Let's rescue the rest of the family."

Steve punted the dinghy across the lake, now

streaked with a reddish gold ribbon from the setting sun. Moments later, he drifted toward the doorway. In the dim light he could barely make out Anna wading through nearly waist-high water. He saw the outlines of the monkeys still perched on the bookcase. "Abandon ship!" he announced as he stepped out of the boat and waded into the house.

"Just in time," Anna said, stuffing toiletries into her knapsack. Steve looked toward a large shelf connected to the bookcase. Pinky and Perky were still standing on it. He had put them there earlier to be above the rising water.

"We know warthogs wallow. But can they swim?" Steve asked.

"I don't know."

"We'll have our hands full holding the monkeys," Steve said. "I'll come back for Pinky and Perky when I get you all safely to the center." He walked over to the bookcase. "Okay, Jack!" Steve clapped. Obediently, the baboon jumped onto Steve's back and encircled his arms around his neck. *EEEEEEEEEE EEEEEEEEEE EEEEEEEEEE.* Max started to scream. Then Flint started to scream. "We're not leaving anyone behind," Anna said, reaching out to pick them up. Flint and Max needed no coaxing as they crawled onto her shoulders.

Steve and Anna carried their precious cargo out to the boat.

Bulu stood at the helm as Steve steadied the tipsy dinghy for Anna. She called softly back to Pinky and Perky, who stood on the shelf looking forlorn. "It's okay. We're coming back for you." Steve climbed in with Jack, then picked up his pole and punted away from the house.

As they floated along, Anna reflected on the splendor of the waterlogged landscape. The bell frogs had started up their orchestra, tinkling like thousands of wind chimes throughout the woodlands. The air was washed and sweet from the blossoming vegetation. Towering pink clouds pushed against the sky. Trees were brushed malachite green. The long grass and reeds waved reflections in the milk-chocolate-colored lake. It was a living watercolor painting.

Anna looked back toward the house. She wondered whether the warthogs felt abandoned. Moments later, when the boat was halfway across the lake, Steve pointed and chuckled. Anna looked to see two little brown icebergs floating a few yards behind the boat. Pinky and Perky were swimming! They were determined to follow. Bulu, standing at the prow, turned his head and spotted them. *Ruff ruff ruff,* he barked, seemingly aware of their momentous achievement. Anna gazed up at Steve punting the boat. The baboon was on his back. "Do you suppose Noah started this way?" she laughed.

⟡

Bap bap bap. A giant moth beat against the glass of a pressure lamp set on a crate beside a bottle of wine and a plate of cheese and crackers. Anna and Steve were too worn out to prepare a meal. Piles of boxes surrounded them in the center's main room. Jack, Flint, and Max had already been fed and were asleep on blankets set atop a crate. Pinky and Perky were lying close by on the cool floor. Bulu was sitting on his haunches next to Anna sharing bits of cheese on crackers.

A crash of thunder broke the silence. The noise woke Max, who screamed and clung to Jack's belly. "It's okay, Max," said Anna softly. At various times when Max was distressed about something, he clung to the underbelly of Jack. At other times, he rode on Bulu's back. Bulu and Jack always seemed to know when Max needed special attention.

For the next week, it rained nearly round the clock. Steve and Anna went about their work at the center, frequently checking the level of the water. The lake was gradually swelling to within thirty yards of the center.

Then one morning, a ray of sunlight caught the mosquito net over the bed. Steve woke and smiled, thinking the rains were at last diminishing. Suddenly the mattress started shaking. It was Bulu on the bed scratching a persistent itch. Lying beside Bulu were the monkeys. They had all slipped under the net and curled up together to sleep. "A bit lonely, hey, guys?" Steve chuckled. He looked over at Anna, sound asleep. Steve yawned and stretched, feeling elation over the bright morning. He pulled back the net and swung his legs out onto the floor.

Splash! His feet hit water. Two inches of it. Stunned, he peered around the room. It looked like a flooding basement. Pinky and Perky were sitting in the water, enjoying their cooling bath. Steve tried not to slip as he walked carefully toward the doorway. Stepping outside, he looked about to see several inches of water encircling the foundation. He walked around the building and was stunned, his eyes riveted on something in the distance. Then he turned and rushed back into the center.

"Anna!" he called as his feet splattered water along the floor. He reached the bed and pulled back the mosquito net. "Oh, Anna."

She woke with a start, sat up, and smiled when she

saw Bulu and the monkeys. Then she spotted the swamped floor and slapped her hand to her forehead.

"We have a little problem," Steve said, heading back to the door. "Come see our house. You won't believe it."

Anna quickly got up, put her feet down in the cold water, and followed. Rounding the building, she looked toward the river. Her jaw dropped. In the distance was what looked like the topside of a surfacing whale. But it wasn't an aquatic mammal. It was their *roof*. The house had disappeared under ten feet of water. "Steve!" She reached for his hand. "Our *home*. Is it ruined?"

Steve shrugged. "We won't know till the water recedes. Let's hope it doesn't get any *deeper*."

Three days later, Steve and Anna's worst fears were coming true. The flood was now rising faster around the wildlife center, which stood like an island in the stream. Inside the building, the rooms were transformed into what Anna dubbed Little Venice. Water had risen six inches on the cement floor. Steve and Anna waded around the room lifting everything onto cinder blocks: the portable stove, the propane tanks, crates, and boxes.

Within a day, Steve had hammered together a couple of makeshift ten-by-ten-foot platforms. They could be raised on cinder blocks as the water level rose. One platform became their living and dining area. The other one became their bedroom. To add to their troubles, their well had collapsed and all the water they used had to be boiled. Jack, Flint, and Max sat glumly on top of piled-up crates watching the flood.

Bulu—who loved the water outdoors—hated getting wet indoors. Especially before going to sleep. Every night, he stared miserably at the flooded rooms. Then he'd jump from crate to crate to hop onto Steve and Anna's bed. Daytime was another matter. Despite the sodden ground, Bulu never missed a chance for a romp into the woodlands with the warthogs. Pinky and Perky found the downpours heavenly, creating a paradise of mud wallows. They pigged out on the new, nutritious

vegetation as if it were an all-you-can-eat buffet. Like all warthogs, Pinky and Perky knelt down to eat when they dug up grass and roots. They were putting on weight fast, growing taller by the day, and gaining more confidence on their own. They seemed to be reaching adulthood overnight.

Because Bulu was spending more time in the

woodlands, Anna worried about him more. The flooded lake would certainly attract crocodiles. And the warthogs' jaunts farther into the bush would catch the attention of lions. But Anna convinced herself that Bulu was gaining experience to be warier of potential danger. At flooded pools, she had observed him standing at the edge watching for any movement. He would wade into the shallow part but avoid venturing into deeper water. He seemed to know that a crocodile could lurk below. Perhaps she was becoming an overprotective mother. After all, Bulu and the warthogs *always* reappeared before the sun went down, nonchalantly walking through the door like farm kids returning from their chores.

One afternoon, Bulu trotted out the center's door into water nearly six inches deep. It was the end of February and the rainy season showed no signs of ending. Pinky and Perky suddenly splashed up behind him, expecting a water chase game. But Bulu ignored them. He turned his head toward the woodlands. Something caught his attention. A shadow moving in the long grass. Then a slight rustling noise. Bulu decided to investigate and waded through the water until he reached solid ground. The woodlands east of the center had so far escaped the flood. He stopped to listen, heard something again, then trotted off and disappeared.

It was early evening when Anna realized she had not seen Bulu since that afternoon. She was lighting the camp stove to begin preparing dinner. By this time, Bulu was always under her feet begging for handouts. As she grabbed a can opener, Steve walked in carrying a cinder block. Jack was riding on his back. "Have you seen Bulu?" she asked, scraping beans from a can.

"Come to think of it, not since after lunch," he said, setting down the block and coaxing Jack off his back. "Don't worry. You know Bulu. Forever snooping about with Pinky and Perky."

Anna nodded and began to put dishes on the dining table atop the platform. She lit candles as Steve took his seat. When they started to eat, Steve cocked his head toward the open door. "Did you hear that?" he said, raising his hand. Anna listened. It was a familiar sound far away. *Aaaaar . . . uummmmph . . . aaaaar . . . uummmmph.* Anna's heart stilled. A moment's silence. Then—*aaaaar . . . uummmmph . . . aaaaar . . . uummmmph*—another one called farther in the distance. "They're at least three miles off," said Steve, trying to put her at ease.

As Steve and Anna ate dinner, they discussed their

workday at the center. But they couldn't stop glancing toward the door. Finally, as Steve filled the teacups, shadows appeared in the dusky light. "You see, I told you so," he announced. "Here they are."

"Thank goodness!" Anna said, seeing Pinky and Perky trotting through the doorway. They were covered with mud and walked over to Steve for their evening scratching. Anna and Steve looked back at the doorway, waiting for Bulu to come strolling in. But after a few moments, there was still no Bulu. "You know how he is," Steve said, trying to convince himself as much as Anna. "Always has to have one more look around before going home."

But fifteen minutes later, it was pitch-black outside. Anna tried to control her dread. "You know he's always home before dark."

Steve turned silent. He had run out of explanations to soothe their worries. He got up from the table and grabbed a flashlight. "I'm going out to look for him."

"*Where?*" Anna shot up from her chair. "*How?*" She threw up her hands in frustration. "In the water? In the dark?" Her outburst awakened Flint and Max, sleeping on a crate. They peered down in alarm.

Steve walked over to a table, opened a steel container, and pulled out his Winchester rifle. He stuffed a handful of cartridges into his belt loops, headed for the door, and stepped outside. The night insects and frogs during the rainy season were deafening. He shone the flashlight toward the trees away from the lake. "BULU!" he called. *"BULU!"* He strained his ears to listen, hoping to hear a bark. Nothing broke the empty silence but the maddening drone of insects. As he headed for the woodlands, he looked back. Anna was framed against the lamplight of the doorway, watching.

Steve waded beyond the edge of the flooding waters, following the flashlight beam. And then he saw Bulu's footprints in the mud, partially erased by warthog tracks. Stepping onto higher ground, he picked up Bulu's trail. The prints led toward the driveway, then went back into the grasses.

Aaaaar . . . uummmmph . . . aaaaar . . . uummmmph. The lions called again. Bulu had not been seen in over seven hours. Steve wondered how far he could have roamed and if he got disoriented in the nearly impenetrable vegetation. "BULU! *BULU!*" he called again. Nothing. He waved his flashlight around the bush. It was choked tight with high grass. There was no way Steve could pick up a trail in it. He stopped to listen again. Then he raised his rifle into the air, pulled the bolt, and squeezed the trigger. *BLAM.* The explosion reverberated among the trees. He stopped to listen for barking. Silence. He fired off two more shots. *BLAM BLAM.* The sound seemed hollow, accentuating the lonely void of an African night. He waited patiently, listening and hoping. The darkness was perforated by hundreds of flashing fireflies. After fifteen minutes or so, Steve reluctantly turned around and retraced his own tracks back.

Anna spotted the beam blinking through the long grass, then stepped off the porch and waded toward the light. She saw that Steve was returning alone and deadly silent. "I'm sure he's just lost," she said as she rushed up to him. "You know how Bulu—" Her lip started to tremble. Then she put her head on Steve's shoulder.

As they walked silently to the center, Steve suddenly stopped. He looked back at the woodlands. Then he moved a short distance from Anna. In anger, he raised the rifle. He fired three shots, pulling the bolt in rapid succession, the shells flying out onto the ground.

A short while later, Steve set up a chair near the door stoop. He took off his muddy boots and put his feet in the cooling water. He held his rifle and flashlight, staring into the blackness. Resting on the bed, Anna tried to comfort herself by cuddling Jack, Flint, and Max. It was past midnight. She soon dozed off, exhausted.

Every so often, Steve beamed the light into the grass. Nothing. He too began to nod. Then, about an hour later, he woke with a start and switched on the flashlight. There was a reflection! Two eyes . . . no . . . four eyes flashed. They were moving . . . seeming to float toward the house. Steve held the light steady. Finally, he could make out the two figures. "Anna! Anna!" he called, getting to his feet.

She bolted upright, confused for a moment, and rushed to the door. She stood beside Steve and saw the reflecting eyes. Anna's mind tried to grasp what the two figures were. Then the recognition. Her baby and a small animal walking alongside. "Bulu!" she yelled, rushing through the water to meet him. "Bulu!" She knelt down in the shallow water and clung to him. Then she looked at the other creature, not quite comprehending for a moment what it was. Steve walked up beside Anna, who was trembling with joy. He knelt down beside her in the water. He cleared his choked throat. "Well, Mister Bulu." He put his hand on the dog's head. "It looks like you brought us a bushbuck."

"It's a baby. A little female. She can't be more than four or five months old," Anna said as Steve held the flashlight on the bushbuck. The tiny calf was barely a foot high.

"Bulu must have flushed her out by accident," Steve said. "Baby bushbucks never venture far from home. Could be a leopard or a lion got her mother."

Anna slowly put out her hand to touch the calf, who showed no fear. The bushbuck stood on legs as thin as sticks, wavering as though she would tip over. "She's so small. Probably not weaned yet."

The calf fascinated Bulu. He began licking her little face, then her long scoop-shaped ears. The bushbuck stood calmly, stretching her head forward to sniff Bulu. She was completely trusting of the gentle dog's attentions.

"Let's get some food into her," Anna said.

Since the water was deeper closer to the center, Steve picked up the calf to carry her inside. Anna rushed about getting a bottle, a rubber glove, and a carton of milk. When Steve set the baby down on the floor, Bulu started nuzzling her. Jack, Flint, and Max, still lying on the bed, raised their heads and spotted the bushbuck. Perhaps because of Bulu's calm attentions to the calf, the vervets did not scream at the intruder. The monkeys quietly observed her, seeing she was not a threat. Pinky and Perky, resting on the floor, got to their feet and stared.

Anna poured the milk into the bottle while Steve cut off the tip of the glove for a nipple. "Let's hope she doesn't reject this," Anna said, knowing the calf could

not survive for long without eating. Steve lifted the baby onto the table. "It feels like she's hollow," he said. As Anna put the bottle to the bushbuck's mouth, she started to suckle instantly—practically inhaling the nipple, white foam streaming down her muzzle. Steve beamed at Anna with relief. While the calf ate, they admired her beauty. Her dark tan coat with white lateral spots was perfect camouflage for bush undergrowth. With her sticklike legs and tiny, frail frame, she looked like a delicate porcelain figurine.

Steve glanced around. A crowd had gathered for the show. Jack, Flint, and Max were sitting in the box seats peering down. Pinky and Perky stood in the front row at his feet. Bulu of course was center stage, standing on the table, tail wagging, licking the calf's ears. Steve chuckled. "What'll be your next orphan, Bulu? An elephant?"

In the succeeding days, the bushbuck drank milk greedily, gaining energy and stamina fast. She followed the dog everywhere. Bulu was remarkably patient, even allowing her to inspect his food bowl.

Steve and Anna had been reading up on bushbucks in a zoology book. They learned one critical fact. The mother bushbuck must lick the baby's anal glands in order for the calf to move its bowels. It was vital to its survival. Yet their little calf never seemed to have a problem. Then one day, the mystery was solved. Steve and

Anna were astounded to see that Bulu had taken over the mother's role. Whenever the bushbuck seemed a bit distressed, Bulu would lick the baby's anal glands, and she would proceed to move her bowels. They knew then that the bushbuck would survive.

"What shall we name her?" Anna asked Steve one evening at the dinner table. Steve gazed down at his feet, where the calf was resting next to Bulu. He thought of the moment he'd first seen the bushbuck as a pair of eyes flashing in the African night. Steve then looked toward the open doorway and smiled. "But of course! Firefly."

The rains remained steady into March. Every day, Steve used a yardstick to check the water level inside the center. The depth had risen to an unsettling thirteen inches. But then one morning in mid-March, something happened.

"The water's dropping!" Steve said when he put the yardstick in the middle of the room.

Anna, eating breakfast, looked down from the dining platform. "Are you sure?"

"A half inch in an hour." Steve pointed to the yardstick. "If the rains up in the hills are ending, we may soon see dry ground. And return to live in the house."

"Hallelujah!" Anna laughed. "To think we can have a real toilet again and not a bush."

For the next few days, the water receded fast. And just in time. Cabin fever had begun to take its toll on the family. Being cooped up in the center day after day was getting on everybody's nerves, man, woman, dog, and monkey alike. Steve and Anna started to grouse at each other over the pettiest matters. Even sweet-natured Bulu turned ugly when Pinky and Perky walked too close to his food. One day, he caught them actually sneaking food from his bowl on the platform. *Big* mistake. Bulu instantly turned into an enraged Tasmanian devil. He flashed his teeth and growled deeply. Pinky and Perky quickly backed off as Bulu morphed from dog to tiger. He stalked forward and bared his canine weapons. The warthogs turned tail and ran out the door. *Bulu* was the boss.

Or so he thought, anyway, until the monkeys challenged him. Flint, Max, and Jack loved watching Bulu squabble with Pinky and Perky over food. During the past weeks, the monkeys had been gradually gaining more confidence. Then one day, for the first time in their lives, they discovered what fun was. It all started when Bulu had his head buried in his bowl. Suddenly a little hand reached in and snatched a morsel. Bulu was outraged! He turned his head and saw the culprit. It was Flint. Bulu instantly gave chase . . . just as the two other monkeys moved in and grabbed handfuls of food. Flint easily outran Bulu, flying up onto the highest crate. Then Max and Jack jumped up to join Flint.

EEEEEEEEEE EEEEEEEEEE EEEEEEEEEE. The monkeys were screaming at the top of their lungs. Not out of fear this time, but out of sheer joy over their prank.

Since they were out of his reach, Bulu stood below barking in frustration. Bristling like a porcupine, he returned to his bowl. As he ate, he kept an eye out for them. But the monkeys were no dummies. They would bide their time. Then they would raid the food bowl again.

The only animal the monkeys didn't tease was Firefly. They seemed to understand her fragility. Only Bulu tried to play gently with the calf. Outdoors, Bulu would lick her face, then playfully run away from her. Firefly would take off after him. Wherever Bulu went, the little bushbuck was there right beside him, never letting him out of her sight. Steve and Anna noticed that the calf was beginning to nibble on the new vegetation surrounding the woodlands. They concluded that she was now certainly six months old, the age when bushbucks are weaned.

Toward the end of March, the river had dropped by several feet. Each day, the "lake" receded farther and farther from the center. Much to Anna and Steve's relief, the floor had now completely dried out.

One night, Anna sat by lantern light under a mosquito net at the worktable. Bulu was at her feet next to Firefly. It was around midnight. Not able to sleep, she decided to work on display designs for the center. Because of the stifling humidity, she left the door and windows wide open. Suddenly Bulu started growling. He stood and faced the open door. The short hair on his back was standing straight up.

Anna pulled the net aside to see. Something caught her eye at the threshold of the door. She froze. A large snake raised its head and looked straight at her. Bulu growled again. Anna knew she must not make any sudden movements, but she had to restrain the dog. Slowly, she moved her hands forward till they partly encircled Bulu's chest. The snake lowered its head, then slid into the room along the wall and disappeared behind boxes.

"Steeeve . . . *Steeeve.*" She spoke softly so as not to alarm the monkeys asleep in their cages.

"What?" a groggy voice answered.

"There's a very *serious* snake in here."

A flashlight winked on beside the bed. "Where?"

"It went behind the boxes. To the left of the door."

"What *kind* of serious?"

"*Cobra* serious. About six feet long."

"Oh, great." Steve got up and slipped on his pants and boots. "I'll put the animals in the truck."

Anna held on to Bulu, his stare fixed on the boxes. Firefly was awake, alerted by Bulu's growling. Anna looked over at the far end of the room. Fortunately, Pinky and Perky were sound asleep.

Steve pointed the flashlight at the boxes stacked fifteen feet away from the doorway. The light probed into the shadows. Nothing. The only thing worse than seeing a deadly snake inside your house is losing sight of it. Where was it? Steve thought a moment. If he and Anna could tread carefully without making any sudden movements, they might be able to get the animals safely past the boxes. Then he would return to search for the cobra.

"Okay, let's go," Steve said as he picked up Firefly. Anna lifted Bulu and gripped him tight, thinking he might try to break free. He growled as they inched along in the dim lantern light. Nearing the door, he started to growl deeper. When they crossed the threshold, Steve cast the flashlight onto the truck and hurried toward it. He opened the rear door and set Firefly on the backseat. Anna put Bulu beside the bushbuck and closed the door. Then she and Steve headed back to the center. The beam of the flashlight searched along the threshold.

Steve leaned into the doorway, aiming the light toward the pile of boxes. No sign of the snake.

Moving forward, they stepped silently toward the cages. Thankfully, the monkeys were still asleep. Steve picked up one cage while Anna lifted the other. Just as they headed toward the door, they suddenly halted. The cobra's head appeared from behind a box! The lantern light caught the glint of its glassy eyes, black, cold, and lethal like an assassin's. Its unblinking stare zeroed in on Steve and Anna. Now they saw that it was a black-banded spitting cobra, one of the deadliest snakes in Africa. They were well aware of its reputation for aggressiveness, especially when it feels threatened or trapped. There's nothing a person can do in a situation like this except freeze.

For what seemed like an eternity, the snake stared. Then it finally lowered its head. Its dark gray body began to flow along the wall. The cobra raised its head again slightly as its six-foot length slid out the door and disappeared. Steve and Anna looked at each other and let out their breath. They knew that this encounter would not be their last. Living close to such fearsome snakes was something they had to come to terms with in Luangwa.

Catfish flopped in the shallow, muddy pool covering the floor of the bush house. Since the structure was on lower ground than the center, it was taking longer for the water to recede from around the foundation. Bulu splashed over to a fish and started pawing at it. "Find a toy, Bulu?" Anna laughed, standing in the middle of the house, holding a wriggling one by its tail.

"Not a pretty face," Steve said, plopping another catfish into a bucket. Its long, rubbery whiskers and wide mouth gave it a somewhat feline look. "That makes twelve we've caught so far."

Anna looked around the room, discouraged. Mud was caked on everything. "It will take forever to clean this up. Where do we begin?"

Steve shrugged as he picked up the bucket and walked outside. His boots stuck in the muck as he slogged to the river to release the fish. All around him, the lush lime-green landscape looked like it had been sprayed with brown graffiti. Day after day as the lake retreated, it left mud plastered about everywhere. On tree trunks, bushes, the long grass.

But if Steve and Anna disliked the sludge, the monkeys simply *hated* it. The long bout of cabin fever finally coaxed Jack, Flint, and Max to venture outside. But the mud was *nasty*. Their feet sank in it, and they lost their ability to play pranks on the dog.

Bulu now had the upper hand and took full advantage. He gleefully romped through the mire with Pinky and Perky, leaving the monkeys far behind. Even Firefly was able to step easily through the mud with her pointed little hooves. She had become Bulu's shadow. Like three little sissies, Jack, Flint, and Max stretched their arms high in the air, tiptoeing through the slop. *Eeeeeeeee eeeeeeeee eeeeeeeee.* Screaming as their legs sank deeper, screwing up their little faces like bawling babies. They soon gave up and returned to solid ground inside the center. Then the stick-in-the-muds sat together on a table, peering out the window at Bulu's antics.

By mid-April, the ground slowly began to dry. Like a chameleon, the river was gradually turning from brown to pale blue, mirroring clearer skies. The water level, at long last, had dropped a few feet below the embankment.

Pinky and Perky had finally moved into their concrete burrow. When Steve first introduced them to the man-made den, they refused to go inside. But when Bulu walked in to check it out, the warthogs did too. Now they slept there every night.

Each day, Pinky and Perky ventured deeper into the bush. Anna and Steve suspected they were roaming farther because they had found boyfriends. If the girls had mated, they would be expecting babies in late September or October. Then one morning, Anna and Steve's suspicions were confirmed. They had just stepped outside the center when they noticed something swaggering out of the woodlands. A young warthog boar—a dashingly handsome suitor who'd come courting for the ladies. He had wavy wiry hair, a large head, protruding warts, and matching upturned tusks like a handlebar mustache. Pinky and Perky had already spotted him and were sashaying across the open ground to say hello.

Suddenly something shattered the boar's cool. It was Bulu. *RUFF RUFF RUFF RUFF.* He streaked across the ground toward the porky Romeo. The boar stopped and stared as the white meteor barreled straight for him. Bulu skidded to a halt barely six feet away, barking in a frenzy of aggression. When the boar started to move forward, Bulu stood his ground and blocked the way.

"BULU! BULU!" Steve and Anna yelled. But their calls fell on deaf ears. They watched helplessly as Bulu

confronted the 150-pound boar. The warthog started tossing his head, making threat displays. Bulu bared his teeth and rumbled a growl. It was a standoff. The heavyweight versus the featherweight. They glowered at each other. Then the boar blinked. He backed off and turned toward the woodlands. He gave one last toss of his head, looked back at the dog with the heart of a honey badger, and retreated into the woods. Pinky and Perky were crestfallen.

Anna had to laugh at Bulu as he stormed back to the house. He was owlish-eyed and still steamed.

Grrrrrrrrr. Sputtering and muttering like a doting dad protecting his teenage daughters. He halted and kicked dirt back with his hind legs as though to shake off the riffraff from the woodlands.

—◆—

The river continued to drop faster throughout late April, but the road was still impassable. This kept Steve and Anna cut off from "civilization," but at least they could now spend their evenings outdoors—and build campfires under the stars.

Bulu resumed his sunset ritual of sitting by the embankment watching for elephants. He had a companion now at his side. Firefly. The monkeys were not yet comfortable being outside in the dark and stayed inside the center. Pinky and Perky always wandered back to their concrete den just before nightfall.

One evening, Anna and Steve sat in the gazebo enjoying dinner. A short time before sunset, Bulu had strolled off to sit at the riverbank. Firefly followed him. Just as Anna lit lamps, Bulu appeared in the shadows with the bushbuck. He was shaking his head continuously as he walked up to the gazebo. Then he began rubbing his face on the ground and scratching his left eye as though trying to shake something off. Anna picked up a lantern and looked at his eye. It appeared to be okay.

"I think an insect bit him," she said as she returned to her chair. But a few minutes later, Bulu started whimpering. She became worried. She grabbed a flashlight and knelt down beside him for a better look . . . and was shocked to see his left eye was swelling. And the other one was watering. Then the chilling realization. "Oh my God, Steve!" she shouted. "I think Bulu's been attacked by a cobra!"

Steve got to his feet and rushed over. "Maybe a scorpion stung him?"

"Let's get him inside to look."

Steve picked up Bulu and carried him to the center. Firefly followed closely behind. Inside, he placed Bulu on a table and Anna pumped a pressure lamp. Aiming his flashlight close, Steve saw that Bulu's left eye was swelling fast. The right eye, though not swollen, was totally bloodshot. "Only a spitting cobra could do this," Steve said. "Might be that same snake that got in here before. We've got to start flushing his eyes *now*."

The loud voices had awakened the monkeys in their cages. They stared quietly, seemingly puzzled by the fuss over the dog. As Anna poured water into plastic bottles, Steve gently put Bulu on his right side in order to give immediate attention to the left eye. As she held open his eyelid, Steve started pouring water directly onto the cornea. Bulu yelped and struggled to get away. But Steve continued to flush the eye for several minutes. Then they turned him over to attend to his right eye. The situation was critical. Spitting-cobra venom is rich in cytotoxins, which cause mucous membranes to hemorrhage. Steve and Anna knew it could lead to irreversible blindness if the poison entered the body through the optic nerve. Even death.

Anna felt a prickle of foreboding crawl over her. She vividly recalled one rainy night a year ago when she and Steve turned up the driveway. The headlights caught a young bushbuck standing by the house. When they got out of the Land Rover, they were surprised that it didn't flee. When they walked closer, they could see its eyes swollen shut, mucus streaming down its face. The bushbuck was blind. Certainly a cobra had attacked it.

After another fifteen minutes, Steve and Anna stopped flushing the eyes. Then they applied antihistamine and antibiotic ointments. Although Bulu was in pain, they couldn't give him aspirin. It acts as a blood thinner and would make the eyes hemorrhage more. There was nothing else they could do for him now. It was going to be a long night.

By morning, Bulu's left eye had swollen completely shut. Mucus had to be continuously wiped from his face. When Steve tried to open the eyelid, Bulu screamed in pain. Steve tried again and was able to keep the lid open a moment. The eye had started to cloud over. Steve and Anna sat in their chairs, feeling helpless watching Bulu on the table in misery.

"We've got to get him to a vet!" Anna pleaded.

Steve took her hand. "The bridge is gone. The road is impassable."

Anna nodded, resigned to the cold facts. She reached out and put her hand on Bulu's chest. When his tail started to wag slightly, she burst into tears. "Steve, I couldn't stand it if he went blind. I'd rather he—" She put her hand to her mouth, shoved away her chair, and ran outside.

By afternoon, Bulu's condition remained the same. Steve dreaded trying to reopen his eyelid, knowing Bulu would scream out. But he needed to see how it was progressing. When he did get it open, he saw the eye had clouded more. Anna reapplied ointments, hoping against hope that the salve alone would heal Bulu.

To take a break from his vigil, Steve stepped outside

with his tea to get air. As he sipped, he thought he heard something. He cocked his head. Then he smiled and ran back inside.

"Anna, did you hear it?"

"Hear what?"

"The *boat*. It's ZAWA!" Steve turned and raced back out the doorway.

Steve stood on the riverbank waving his arms as the ZAWA patrol boat rumbled around the bend. He recognized Njovu in the front, steering the boat that carried five armed rangers. Moments later, the launch chugged up to the bank as a ranger threw out a mooring rope. Steve tied it to a log. Njovu idled the engine and snapped a salute. "No worry, Mister Steve." Njovu chuckled. "I not bring you another monkey. We on patrol."

"Njovu! Am I glad to see you!" Steve shouted. "We have an emergency. I need to get to Lusaka. The dog's been attacked by a cobra."

Less than thirty minutes later, Steve was back on the riverbank with his suitcase. Anna stood beside him, holding Bulu. Firefly was at her feet. "Njovu's kindly leaving one of his rangers with you as a guard," Steve said. "I think I can just make the last flight out of Mfuwe." He turned and kissed Anna. Then he reached over to cradle Bulu, wrapped in a blanket. Anna hugged and kissed them both.

"I'll take good care of the rest of the family," Anna said, showing a brave face. Steve stepped carefully into the boat and Njovu gave the shove-off sign to the ranger left behind. The engine revved and sputtered into reverse; then the boat turned and roared against the current.

Anna stood silently. Firefly stepped closer to the bank and watched the boat move farther away. As it started to reach the bend, Anna saw Steve turn and wave. She waved back. Then she knelt down beside the little bushbuck and put her arms around her. She wondered whether it would be the last time she'd ever see Bulu. "Godspeed," she whispered as the boat disappeared.

Bulu lay shivering under a blanket on Steve's lap in the backseat of a taxi. It was morning rush hour in downtown Lusaka. Horns blasted along crowded Cairo Road. Steve held Bulu's paws to prevent him from scratching at his eyes. The taxi careened onto a side street and pulled up in front of the veterinary clinic. As Steve rushed into the reception room with Bulu in his arms, he ran into a woman in a white jacket. It was the veterinarian.

"A *cobra*," Steve blurted out. "It got him in the eyes."

The startled doctor looked at Steve, then at the dog with the mucus streaming from his eyes. "Quick, come this way," she said.

Steve followed the vet into the examining room and laid Bulu on the steel table.

"How long ago was he attacked?" she asked, putting on latex gloves.

"About forty-eight hours. I had to fly here from South Luangwa."

"Hmmm." She sighed, turning on a bright light above her. "Immediate treatment is critical for snake venom." She adjusted the light closer to Bulu's face. His left eyelid was swollen shut like a prizefighter's. She placed her fingertips on each side of the eye to open it. Bulu screamed in agony. Steve held him tightly.

"His left eye has gone cloudy white," she observed. "There are also deep ulcers on the cornea. The right eye is not so bad. But pressure can build up inside the eyeball and actually rupture it."

She stepped back a moment and noticed the stricken look on Steve's face. "I can't guarantee I can save his sight or his life. I can operate on the corneas for the ulcers." She put her hand on Steve's shoulder. "I'll do everything I can."

It was late afternoon when Anna stepped out of the center with a thermos and a sack of snacks. She headed for the river. The monkeys and the bushbuck followed closely. A few moments later, she walked into the gazebo and sat down. "It's okay, Firefly. I think Bulu will come back." Anna cupped the silky muzzle of the bushbuck in her hand. Firefly's eyes, like auburn pools, looked trustingly up at her.

Anna glanced over to the spot where Bulu always watched for the elephants. Jack, Flint, and Max jumped up on the table to eat their treats. She smiled as Jack broke off a piece of dried pineapple and passed it to Max. The baboon never failed to share every meal with the shy little vervet.

Earlier in the day, Anna had worked on her anti-poaching display at the center. But she could hardly concentrate, thinking about Bulu. It had been over a week since Steve had left for Lusaka. As she petted Firefly, Anna continually glanced upstream, waiting and watching. The ZAWA guard stood a hundred feet away, resting his rifle. One evening, he had spied a leopard prowling close to the tent he'd set up near the center. Anna was grateful for his presence. Not just for her own safety, but for Firefly's and the monkeys'.

"Madam!" the guard shouted as he pointed upstream. "I hear boat."

Anna took a deep breath, got to her feet, and walked toward the guard. She stood beside him, her pulse racing. As the engine noise got louder, the hippos across the river started to grumble. Only their heads were visible, all turned in the direction of the sound. A moment later, the ZAWA launch roared into view and the hippos submerged. Anna could see the outline of four human figures in the boat. When the launch got within two hundred feet of the bank, she saw Steve sitting in the back. The engine spluttered and slowed as it drew closer. When the boat pulled up, a man threw out a rope to the guard on the bank. Then Anna's heart sank. Steve was sitting *alone*! She ran frantically up to the launch and cried out, "Where's Bulu?"

Steve's face split into a grin. He lifted a blanket off a box at his feet. Anna was confused. All she saw in it was a white cone. Then she spotted Bulu's head—inside the cone! "Oh, Bulu!"

"Miss Anna," Njovu called over the chugging engine. "We bring dog—" He looked back at the box, then corrected himself and smiled. "No. We bring *Master Bulu* home to you."

The guard steadied the boat as Steve climbed out cradling Bulu in his arms. The dog's eyes were moist with salve but no longer cloudy. Bulu barked as soon as he saw Anna. "He can see me!" She burst into tears, trying to hug him but his cone collar kept getting in her way. Then she laughed from sheer joy.

"The operation on the eye ulcers was a success," Steve said. "But we're not out of the bush yet. There's a ton of medicine in my bag. You can forget about sleeping. *Every* half hour we've got to give it to him. For three weeks!"

Anna turned to Njovu with heartfelt gratitude. "Thank you, thank you, Njovu. You have been a guardian angel."

"Can you and your men stay for dinner?" Steve urged.

"We like very much," Njovu said. "But we must return to base after guard pack up tent."

"Then we insist on a rain check," Anna said.

Njovu made a point of looking up at the cloudless sky, and everyone chuckled.

Minutes later, the guard ran back with his tent and equipment. He climbed into the launch as another ranger set Steve's bag on the bank. "We must go now," Njovu said, revving the engine. The rope was thrown back in and the boat reversed, then rumbled forward. Njovu gave a wave over his shoulder as he swerved the launch upriver.

Bulu started to squirm, so Steve set him down on the bank. Because of the cone, he had to raise his head high to see up. He sniffed the air. Anna nudged Steve and pointed behind him. The rest of the family was gathering. Jack, Flint, and Max were moving closer ever so cautiously. Getting within twenty feet, they sat down and stared, eyes blinking rapidly. They were perplexed by Bulu's appearance.

The rear part of the dog looked like Bulu, but why the creepy cone head? When Bulu walked toward them, they backed off. Firefly, though, stepped calmly up to the dog and sniffed. Then she stuck her nose inside the cone to lick his face. Bulu practically wagged his rear end off. Then he trotted along the bank, followed by the bushbuck. He reached his favorite place next to the mopane tree and sat down.

Steve and Anna had decided to have supper on the riverbank. They set up the table and chairs and built a campfire. Just before sunset, Steve lit the fire and Anna made cheese sandwiches. When all was ready, Jack hopped onto Steve's lap, while Flint and Max jumped onto Anna's shoulders. The monkeys had finally accepted that the cone creature was really Bulu.

Anna opened a bottle of wine. "We have something to celebrate tonight."

Steve chuckled as he observed Bulu. "It looks like he's using a megaphone."

At the riverbank, the white cone was moving to the left and right. Anna put her hand to her mouth and giggled. "What better way to call the elephants?"

For the next three weeks, Steve and Anna sleepwalked through the night like the parents of a newborn. They worked in shifts. Every half hour salve had to be applied to Bulu's eyes. But all the attention did the trick. At the end of three weeks, Bulu's eyes had cleared completely. Finally, they could remove the lamp-shade collar.

Steve and Anna stood with Bulu outside the center with Jack, Flint, Max, and Firefly. As Steve cut the wire holding the cone, it dropped off like a termite wing. Suddenly gaining his peripheral vision, Bulu was stunned for a second. He looked to his left and to his right. He growled a bit. He flew into one of his crazy spells, running around and around, huffing and puffing, tearing up the turf. He fixed his sights on Jack, Flint, and Max. *Eeeeeeeee eeeeeeeee eeeeeeeee.* The monkeys picked up on the game and raced across the open ground, disappearing behind the house, the dog hot on their trails. "GO, BULU. *GO!*" Steve and Anna cheered him on. Bulu was back to being Bulu.

By mid-May, the bush house was again becoming livable. Under cloudless violet skies, Steve continued to make repairs on the roof thatch and the reed walls. The sun gradually baked the dampness and mold from the dwelling. Inside, Anna scrubbed everything clean, unpacked boxes, shelved food items, and hung curtains. Steve and Anna felt their lives were returning to normal. Soon Mabvuto and a couple of the workers would return to help prepare the center for its grand opening.

The cool breeze of the mornings was exhilarating, especially for Bulu. He loved trotting off into the woodlands with Firefly, who was attracted to the rich vegetation. Because Pinky and Perky were becoming more independent, Bulu took the little bushbuck under his wing. They were becoming inseparable.

The floods had postponed Steve and Anna's schedule for the opening of the wildlife center by several weeks. The timetable of the elephants had also been upset. Usually by March the herds had migrated from the hills to the river to feed on the flourishing vegetation. But the swamped valley had delayed their journey. Now hundreds of elephants were back at the river and scattered throughout the woodlands, feasting on the thriving grasses. Pregnant females would be dropping their calves soon after a gestation period of nearly two years.

But the new, dense undergrowth makes the bush a dangerous place for all wild animals. Traps become invisible. Taking advantage of the situation, meat poachers set thousands of snares in the thick brush. Fishermen put more wires along riverbanks and lagoons. Although most snares are meant for small antelope, larger animals get caught too—buffalo, zebras, giraffes, elephants. Once a leg gets entangled, the wire noose cuts into the flesh, tightening deeper and deeper to the bone. If an elephant's trunk becomes ensnared, the tip of it is severed. Wounds fester quickly in the damp tropical air, causing the animal to die from the spreading infection. Larger traps, made of steel cable, can strangle a lion or a leopard as it thrashes desperately to tug itself free. It can take days of unspeakable agony, and raging thirst, before an animal finally dies.

Steve and Anna worried about Bulu getting caught in a snare. But there was little they could do to discourage his bush jaunts. They couldn't stop Bulu from being Bulu.

Mabvuto pedaled his bicycle along the dirt road that cut a brown swath through the emerald woodlands. He was heading for the wildlife center. He had to maneuver carefully to avoid the deep tire ruts that had dried hard in the sun like pottery. And then he saw something in the middle of the road that made him skid to a halt. Fresh, wet elephant dung.

He stood silently, gripping the handlebars tight, looking to the right and left. The morning sun cast gray shadows across the way. The six-foot-high grass between the trees obstructed his view. Mabvuto knew how fast an elephant could charge. And how silently it could walk on its thick padded feet. He had once surprised a bull at a turn in the road and barely escaped the enraged trumpeting tusker. He was aware that the females would be testy guarding their newborns. Mabvuto listened, hearing only his pulse pounding in his ears. After a few minutes, he put his feet on the pedals and pumped madly on down the road.

A half hour later, Mabvuto met up with an obstruction. A gully about thirty feet wide. He got off his bike to check whether he could get across. No water flowed along it, but the floods had left behind a seemingly bottomless vat of mud. Logs and huge branches stuck up out of the surface like skeletons in a tar pit. Buffalo and giraffes had left deep hoofprints in the edges of the black glue. They had not dared venture into the middle. Mabvuto was frustrated. It might not dry up for a couple of weeks. He walked farther along the mud alley embankment. Then he spied something. A large tree had fallen across the channel. It was like a bridge. Mabvuto smiled. He just might be able to carry his bike and knapsack to the other side if he stepped carefully along the trunk. Encouraged, he rushed back to get his stuff.

Bulu was walking with Firefly from behind the center when he spotted Mabvuto pedaling his bike up the driveway. *Ruff ruff ruff ruff.* Bulu ran toward him, his tail wagging excitedly. "Ah! Bulu!" Mabvuto called out as he coasted up to the entryway. Reaching down to pet him, he was surprised to see a bushbuck standing calmly beside the dog.

Steve and Anna rushed out the door. "Mabvuto! Welcome back!"

Anna gave him a big hug. When Steve shook his hand, Mabvuto did a double take. "Mister Steve . . . there's a . . ."

"Baboon on my back?" Steve laughed. "Let me introduce you to Jack."

Without hesitation, Mabvuto put his fingers forward. Jack looked directly into his eyes. When the baboon's little hand encircled the young man's fingers, Mabvuto's face lit up like a kid's.

Bulu was watching. He stepped forward to paw at Mabvuto's leg for attention. "Bulu very jealous." Mabvuto chuckled as he knelt down to pet him. Then Firefly stepped forward to get her ears stroked.

Anna smiled, observing there was something special about this gentle, bright young man. Animals were drawn to him. His attitude encouraged her. If more villagers could learn sensitivity toward animals, there was hope for Luangwa's wildlife.

Mabvuto suddenly reached into his knapsack and pulled out a piece of paper. "My driving license!" he announced proudly. Then he held up another certificate. "I know how to fix truck too."

A week later, Steve and Mabvuto were finishing up the last repair work to the bush house. They were standing outside under the two water barrels cleaning the pipes that connected to the sink, toilet, and shower. Mud left behind by the floods had clogged the lines. As Steve tightened a bolt, Anna walked up beside him. "Firefly's sick."

"What's wrong?" he asked.

"She's got diarrhea. I found her lying under some brush."

"Where's she now?"

"Near the river. Come and see."

Steve followed Anna. About two hundred feet away, they found Bulu standing beside a bush. Firefly was underneath, lying on her side, almost invisible in the dappled shade. At first glance, Firefly looked fine. She seemed to have gained weight. But when Steve and Anna knelt down to pet her, they saw her belly was bloated, rising and falling fast under duress from the diarrhea.

"I wonder what—" Anna interrupted herself. She remembered once witnessing a similar situation back in England. She stood up and looked at Steve. "I think Firefly may be dying."

"*What?*"

"I think she's got a condition common to ruminant animals," Anna said. "Gases build up in the four compartments of the stomach. I saw this with livestock in England. They often overeat lush vegetation in the spring. It causes bloat." She gestured around at the luxuriant grasses. "The diarrhea is usually fatal."

"What can we do?" Steve asked.

"Probably not much. The diarrhea's dehydrating her fast," Anna answered in a hollow voice. "I can give her tea. Sometimes the tannin in it counteracts poisons in various plants."

Minutes later, Anna returned with a thermos. She sat down beside Firefly, who was becoming more and more listless. Steve tried to comfort the bushbuck by stroking her back. Bulu continued to stand close by, watching. Firefly turned her head away whenever Anna attempted to spoon the tea. The bushbuck was too exhausted to drink. Firefly was fading before their eyes.

Anna gently picked her up and cradled her in her arms. Completely dehydrated, she felt as light as papier-mâché.

Jack, Flint, and Max were playing chase games outside the house. But they became curious when Bulu did not join them. They walked over to where Bulu stood. Max was particularly silent, staring at the bushbuck. Firefly always let him ride on her back.

By late afternoon, Firefly went into spasms, her spindly legs starting to shake. Anna never left her, holding her close. Then the bushbuck shuddered one last time, her legs stiffened outward, and her back arched. Her soulful eyes glazed over. Firefly was gone.

Anna sat for a while holding the bushbuck. Bulu had lain down close beside. Then Anna placed Firefly on the ground and walked to the house. Bulu followed, but he kept looking back to where Firefly lay.

Anna and Steve decided that they must let nature take its course. They chose not to bury the bushbuck, but rather to leave her under a tree near the riverbank. Certainly a scavenger would see the body and carry out nature's plan.

Wanting to be alone, Anna walked out of the house and returned to the bush where Firefly lay. She picked up the little bushbuck and carried her several hundred yards along the riverbank to a large mahogany tree. There she set Firefly gently under its spreading branches. She stood silently a moment, then strolled on about fifty yards upriver to a grove of trees overlooking the bank. When she sat down, she reflected on the privilege of living close to wild animals. She remembered the words of the writer Karen Blixen, who had a bushbuck named Lulu that often visited Blixen's farm in Kenya: "Lulu came in from the wild world to show that we were on good terms with it, and she made my house one with the African landscape, so that nobody could tell where the one stopped and the other began."

As Anna watched the sun dip behind the trees, she looked back at the mahogany. She was surprised to see a small white animal standing under it. It was Bulu. Anna did not move, wanting to watch him secretly. Unaware of her presence, Bulu stood as the sun went down. He turned his head at various sounds in the bush but did not pursue them. He just stayed there, silent and still, watching over the bushbuck's body. Anna wondered, did Bulu feel something for the dead Firefly? She thought so. She believed it was a reverence for life.

Boom . . . *boom.* Bulu heard the distant gunshots and ran out the door, barking. Steve and Anna, sitting at the breakfast table, recognized the sound of muzzle loaders. They rushed outside to listen. *Boom . . . boom.*

"There's at least four of them," Steve said, knowing that the handmade rifles take a minute to reload. "The gang could be bigger. They're probably after buffalo or elephants."

"The shots seem to have come from the south," Anna said.

They hurried to the Chowo to check. Reaching the viaduct, they stood and listened. Then . . . *boom.* Bulu started to bark again.

"Sounds like they're about a half mile away," Anna said. "Down the Luangwa."

Steve looked south across the broken bridge where its center had collapsed. To the left of the viaduct, the mud was too deep for a vehicle. He looked to the right to observe the hundred-foot-wide pool, the size of a small reservoir. It was about all that was left of the shrinking Chowo, draining along a channel into the Luangwa. Steve thought a moment. "I'm going for the boat," he said. "I've got to find the poachers' location to alert ZAWA and the Rapid Action Team rangers."

"You said the gang could be *big*. I'm going with you." She set her jaw determinedly.

"Okay." Steve nodded. "I'll have Mabvuto help with the boat and the outboard."

"Great," Anna said. "I'll get the rifle and throw a knapsack together." She turned and headed for the house. Bulu trotted after her.

Minutes later, the Land Rover pulled up to the bank near the bridge. Steve and Mabvuto lifted the dinghy and small outboard engine off the truck. Steve first needed to see whether the Chowo was deep enough to navigate. If so, he and Anna could easily glide along it, then lower the outboard in the deeper water found midstream in the Luangwa.

Before entering the pool, he checked the surface. He was cautious. The previous year an old bull hippo had taken over the area as his territory. The water was murky. Trees and brush overhung the banks of the channel, casting shadowy reflections. Steve picked up a big stick and threw it into the center to see whether anything would surface. He waited a few moments, watching. Nothing. Then he tossed off his shoes, slipped along the side of the bank, and plunked into mud up to his ankles. The pool seemed to be shallower than it looked. Like stepping into molasses, he slowly waded into water up to his shins. "It might be deeper farther along," he called back to Mabvuto. "I'll check it out."

Ruff ruff ruff ruff. Bulu was climbing down the bank. "Oh no," Steve said. "I don't need you tagging along." Not to be cheated of adventure, Bulu slowly waded in the shallow water. The muck sucked at his feet, making him walk stiff-legged like a robot dog. Then he stopped, suspicious of the depth in the middle of the pool. He cautiously scanned the water to the left and right.

Watching Bulu struggle to move forward, Steve realized how vulnerable they'd be if the hippo was still hanging around. Fortunately, there was no sign of the old bull. Steve waded down the middle of the channel in the direction of the Chowo's mouth. Bulu followed slowly.

Several hundred feet farther along, Steve was encouraged when he walked into water up to his thighs. The depth was sufficient for the dinghy. He peered behind him. Bulu was now swimming. Steve was surprised he was still following since Bulu was so guarded about deep water. Steve looked through the tunnel of brush and could just make out the Luangwa about two hundred yards ahead. But there was one obstruction to his left. A fallen tree bridged the channel about fifty yards in front. The center of the tree appeared to be a few feet above the water. The boat might be able to slip under it. He had to investigate.

Wading within forty yards of the tree, he felt a sloping sandbar beneath his feet. It brought him back up to ankle level. Bulu was now standing on it too, completely still, his eyes suddenly fixed on something ahead. It was the fallen tree. Steve studied it. There were ripples underneath it. They appeared to be caused by branches and dead leaves hanging from the trunk.

"It's okay, Bulu," he said. "Only a few bran—" *Grrrrrrrrrrr.* Bulu started his long, low, deep growl. Steve's blood went cold. Bulu had definitely seen something. Steve knew they must get out of the water *at once.* Standing in the middle of the channel, he looked to his left. The bank was too steep, with no footholds. He looked to his right. He spotted the gnarled roots from a decaying tree sticking out of the crumbling bank like rungs on a ladder. If they could reach the roots in time, it might be possible to climb out. Steve knew he must remain calm without making any sudden movements that would attract whatever lay beneath the fallen tree. At least the water was shallow where they stood. The tree roots were about seventy feet away.

"Come on, Bulu, let's go." Continuing to growl, Bulu stuck beside Steve, heading toward the right bank. Much to Steve's alarm, the sandbar began to slope downward, taking him deeper and deeper. Bulu was already swimming when Steve found himself in water above his waist. Worse yet, the sand was now mixed with muck. Each footfall felt as though he was walking on plungers suctioning the bottom. Fearing his feet would be cemented in the mire, he dared not stop for a second. With great effort, he kept plodding on in slow motion, relying on the measured sweep of his arms to keep moving forward. Bulu stayed close, paddling slowly beside him.

Steve tried not to think of his legs moving under the murk as submerged branches scratched at them. He concentrated totally on reaching the bank. He kept his eyes on the protruding roots until they were within arm's reach. Grabbing for them, he got a hold and started to pull himself up. But he lost his grip and fell back into the stream with a big splash. Thrashing in the water to get a grasp, he tried again. Finally, he was able to get one leg around a lower root to climb up. When he got both feet onto the root for balance, something made him turn his head. Behind him, only fifty feet away, was a spearhead-shaped wake cutting fast through the water! It had a wide snout and was moving straight toward him and Bulu.

"GET OUT, BULU!" he yelled. *"GET OUT! GET OUT!"* Bulu was below the bottom root and confused about where to go. As Steve leaned down with one arm to grab him, Bulu swam toward the bank. Reaching it, he could only get about a yard up, his forepaws slipping, clawing madly at the crumbling earth. Steve clutched the roots and climbed with all his strength, heaving himself over onto the top of the bank. Frantic, he looked back at the water to see a flat, wide green snout and protruding eyes twenty feet away from the roots. It was a huge crocodile!

Bulu was now desperately digging his hind legs into the ground. He finally got a foothold and scrambled up to the top. He whirled around and looked down. Staring up at him were reptilian eyes on a scaly head with jagged, protruding teeth like a great white shark's. Mercifully, the nine-foot-high bank was too steep for the croc. *RUFF RUFF RUFF RUFF RUFF.* Bulu raged at the beast. If there was one thing Bulu hated in this world, it was a crocodile.

Catching his breath, Steve got to his feet. He walked over to Bulu and sat down beside him. Peering over the edge of the bank, Steve saw that the croc had gone. Bulu stopped barking but kept growling with his eyes fixed on the water. Steve heaved a sigh, thinking how quickly they both could have been taken. "I *did* need you tagging along after all." He gazed at Bulu a few moments, then put his arm around him. "You weren't going to leave my side, were you?" Steve clutched him tight. "*No matter what.*"

The following morning, Steve dusted off his old bicycle in the storeroom. He had decided to bike with Mabvuto to ZAWA headquarters to report that poachers were hunting downriver. The tipsy boat was too much of a risk with the croc still lurking about. But Steve was determined to inform the rangers as soon as possible.

By late afternoon, he and Mabvuto had biked to ZAWA and back. As soon as they pedaled up the driveway, Bulu bounded down it to greet them. Anna stepped out of the house carrying a wicker food basket.

"Anna! Good news!" Steve called as he coasted the bike up beside her. "The gullies are drying up fast. By next week, the road should finally be passable."

"Then ZAWA get rangers into bush faster!" Mabvuto added excitedly. "Tomorrow, they bring boat and patrol downriver."

"At long last we can open the center and bring the children," Anna said as she headed for the gazebo.

⬯

As darkness approached, Anna, Steve, and Mabvuto were seated in the gazebo eating dinner. They wanted to be outside to listen for poachers' gunfire. Bulu was their early-warning system. But so far he was quiet, nudging Anna as she removed homemade bread from a basket. Sitting next to Bulu were Jack, Flint, and Max, munching on bits of canned fruit. Mabvuto chuckled as he watched the monkeys. Right on schedule, Jack was chewing up food and handing it to Max. Flint had one arm around Bulu's leg like a buddy. Steve reflected a moment as he observed the pure contentment of the once-traumatized monkeys. "Anna. You know how we've wondered what happens to baby elephants after the horror of seeing their mothers gunned down by poachers?"

Anna nodded. "Are the babies adopted by another herd? Or do they run off into the bush? Wander alone till they die?" Steve's question had triggered something that always haunted them. *The ghosts of thousands of elephant families slaughtered in thirty years.* She looked at Steve. "Sometimes it seems so hopeless. What can anyone do to help them?"

Mabvuto spoke up. "You can bring them *here.*"

Anna and Steve looked at him. *"Here?"*

"The babies. *They have no place to go,*" Mabvuto stressed. He pointed to the monkeys. "That is why they are here, yes?"

Anna and Steve nodded.

"You build house for warthogs," Mabvuto continued. "You build house for baby elephants."

Steve and Anna sat silently. Anna took a sip of wine. "I wonder if we really could?" Steve put his hand on her arm. He raised his eyebrows and grinned. Anna smiled back. The seed had been planted.

Steve pointed to an open space surrounded by trees near the Chowo. "Right over there would be an ideal setting for the structure." He stood up to think. "Building it will be the easy part. The hard part will be *raising* an elephant."

"And handling a traumatized youngster that can

flatten us." Anna put her hand on Bulu. "Or our young friend here."

"We'll need to think this through carefully," Steve said. "Then write a proposal for ZAWA."

Anna hesitated a moment. "Are we crazy to even consider taking this on?"

"Yes. Remember what our friends back in England said when we announced we were flying the coop for Africa?"

Anna smiled, remembering their words.

Steve stretched out his arms along the Luangwa embankment. "And look where it got us!"

For the next few days, Steve and Anna worked on their proposal to ZAWA. The bush house was littered with first drafts. When they'd finally finished typing it up, Mabvuto appeared at the doorway. "Right on time," Steve said as he sealed the envelope and handed it over. "All we can do now is cross our fingers." Mabvuto put the letter in his satchel and headed down the driveway.

Just as Steve started to sit back down— *TWAAANG*—a tin bowl overturned and whirled wildly across the floor, scattering dog food. *EEEEEEEEE.* Flint snatched a fistful of corned beef. *RUFF RUFF RUFF*

RUFF. Bulu instantly gave chase as Flint flew up on top of the bookcase. Shifting to play mode, Bulu lowered his front legs and thrust his butt up in the air. His wagging tail was too much of a temptation for Max. He appeared out of nowhere and pulled it hard. Bulu spun around to chase him as Jack grabbed handfuls of corned beef and joined Flint on the bookcase. Eyes blazing with mischief and mouths stretched wide open, the monkeys let loose shrieking laughs. *EEEEEEEEE EEEEEEEEE EEEEEEEEE.*

Bulu jumped against the bookcase and tried to climb it. *RUFF RUFF RUFF RUFF.* But he slipped backward on the first shelf. This excited the monkeys even more. *EEEEEEEEE EEEEEEEEE EEEEEEEEE.* Anna and Steve cringed. "Please put them outside!" Anna said. When Steve got up, the monkeys *knew* he'd try to stop their game, and no way were they giving up easily.

As Steve reached for the top of the bookcase, all pandemonium broke loose. Jack leapt onto the top of the mosquito net as Flint and Max catapulted themselves onto the pantry shelves, overturning canisters that spilled flour, powdered milk, and sugar. Pots and pans and dishes were launched into space like flying saucers crashing onto the floor. Glass jars of jam and jelly exploded, sending sticky globs of shrapnel everywhere. Anna jumped to her feet. "Flint! Max! No! *Stop it!*" But *no* is not a word in vervet vocabulary.

Jack, meanwhile, had turned the mosquito net into a trampoline. Screaming gleefully, he bounced on the mesh. This was too much fun to miss. Flint and Max leapt from the shelves to the net. Now the three monkeys were jumping around like circus acrobats, stretching the flimsy fabric to its limits. Bulu yowled at their antics frustratingly out of his reach. The quiet little bush house had turned into a carnival.

EEEEEEEEE EEEEEEEEE EEEEEEEEE. Steve and Anna clasped their hands over their ears. The monkeys were having the time of their lives until the net ripped. They fell through the hole and landed back on *Bulu's* turf. Caught off guard, Jack, Flint, and Max madly untangled themselves from shreds of net and scrambled out the door. Bulu shifted into high gear and tore after the pack, disappearing across the open ground. As if standing in the aftermath of a cyclone, Steve and Anna looked around the torn-up room, with glass, cans, and boxes strewn about. Then, in spite of himself, Steve had to grin. "Have you *noticed,* Anna," he said, "how much more *self-assured* the monkeys are?" Anna raised an eyebrow. "Why, yes, Steve, now that you mention it. They have all the grace of the Three Stooges."

One morning several days later, a ZAWA truck came up the driveway. It stopped in front of the house and a ranger stepped out. "Officer Njovu has letter for you," he announced, holding a brown envelope. He handed it over to Steve, who opened it and quickly scanned the text. "Njovu likes our idea!" He waved the letter in the air.

"Wonderful!" Anna's face lit up.

"ZAWA wants to set up a meeting with us." Steve continued reading, then suddenly stopped. He sighed and looked off into the distance. He handed the letter to Anna. She scanned it and her mood turned somber. Steve put his arm around her as she bit her lip, trying to retain composure in front of the officer. "Only a week," she said, looking at Steve. Seemingly resigned to something, she walked back into the house.

The ZAWA letter lay open on the breakfast table. "I knew this was to be expected," she said. "We couldn't hold on to them forever."

"You know it's for the best. Jack, Flint, and Max finally living a life among their own kind." Steve forced a smile. "Rather than living with two retired police officers and a dog." He picked up the letter and read it out loud. " 'A primate rehabilitation program has been initiated in western Zambia. The project will release once-captive baboons and vervets into a nature reserve—after they've bonded with other orphaned monkeys at a wildlife holding facility in Lusaka. This process allows the newly formed simian families to gradually adapt to a natural life in the bush.' "

Anna nodded, then got up to look out the window toward the river. Four small figures sat on the bank. Bulu, Jack, Flint, and Max were watching a hippo lumbering from the shore into the water. She wondered how Bulu would get along without his friends. She turned to Steve. "I'm going to the storeroom to unpack my bike. Tomorrow I'm taking Jack, Flint, and Max for a ride. I need to spend some time with them before they're gone."

"**K**eep your eyes on the road ahead," Steve cautioned Anna as they stood beside the bicycle in front of the house. "It's easy to get distracted and pedal too fast like we did in the Yorkshire dales." He tightened a screw on the bike's front wheel. "There were only hedgehogs to dodge then."

"We'll be fine," Anna said, fastening a small lunch bag to the handlebars. "Won't we, guys?" Bulu gave a little bark. Jack, Flint, and Max sat next to him munching on nuts. Bulu sniffed the wheels and spokes. Then he lifted his leg and peed on the back tire. "Bulu!" Anna laughed as she banged her foot on the kickstand. "Okay, chaps. We're off."

Steve gave her a hug. Anna pedaled slowly away from the house as Bulu followed. She got only a few feet away when—*eeeeeeee eeeeeeee eeeeeeee*—Flint and Max started running alongside her. She chuckled and stopped the bike. "I knew you'd want to come along." She patted her hips. Flint jumped up and climbed onto her shoulder, wrapping his arms tightly around her neck. Then Max leapt onto her lap, clasping his hands onto her waist. Anna looked behind her. "How about you, Jack?" she said. But Jack continued to eat, ignoring her. "You're still a daddy's boy, huh?" She shrugged. *Ruff ruff ruff.* Bulu ran ahead, then circled back to urge Anna to move faster.

As Steve leaned against the doorway, Jack suddenly jumped onto his shoulders. "So, Mister Jack," he said, tickling him under the chin. "Biking isn't your thing?" He smiled as he watched Anna pedal off with her babies, Bulu leading the way.

Shafts of pink light slanted through the trees as Anna pumped along the road. The grasses had been nibbled down by the wildlife, creating a parkland setting of trees on a jade carpet. Bulu ran ahead, nose to the ground. A mile farther on, he halted and stared at some brush. He started to growl.

Anna never ignored Bulu's warnings and coasted to a stop. A couple of shadows flashed between the thorn branches. And then Bulu started to wag his tail. Trotting out of the brush were Pinky and Perky. Bulu rushed over to nuzzle them. They snorted at him, making what sounded like little chuckling noises. But the warthogs had stirred up a squadron of tsetses from the bushes.

"Oh, great," Anna groaned. Bulu snapped his head around to bite at the flies landing on his back.

Knowing that tsetses avoid the direct sun, Anna called out, "Come on!" and began to pedal fast down the road. The monkeys clung to her for dear life, the warthogs raced along on each side of her, and the little white dog dashed along in front. She thought how ridiculous she must look. "Oh boy, Bulu," she hooted. "Can you imagine if anyone saw me now? *Run for your lives! A barmy British woman is loose in Luangwa!*" She steered on around a bend giggling, intoxicated by the cool morning air and the African sun on her face.

Eeeeeeee eeeeeeee eeeeeeee. Anna came to a halt. A troop of forty or so vervet monkeys was streaming across the road about three hundred feet ahead. Bulu stopped, growled slightly, and narrowed his eyes. They were too far away for a chase. Anna had long ago learned to interpret Bulu's language of growls. A soft one meant "time for a game," rasping ones meant "warning," long, low ones meant real trouble. She felt Flint and Max grasp her tighter. They were fearful of their own species, intimidated by the bush where they were born. She remembered why she and Steve came to live in Africa in the first place. To be free. Not to be possessed by anything. And she felt a little guilty, like a hypocrite. She had tried to own these monkeys. She accepted now that Flint, Max, and Jack must be liberated into the wild.

Bulu looked up at her, wondering why the long halt. She balanced herself again and continued on down the road, maneuvering around the deep, dried-up elephant tracks. Bulu often fell behind, stopping here and there to sniff a bush or footprint. Anna's high spirits made her throw caution to the wind and she pumped faster.

As she rounded one curve, thick brush blocked her view ahead. She pedaled onward and suddenly found herself on a collision course with an eleven-foot-high gray mountain blocking her way. A bull elephant!

Startled, the creature whirled around with ears unfurled, trunk swinging, its scream splitting the sky. *UUUURRRRRR.* She skidded to a halt, losing control of the handlebars and falling onto the road. Adrenaline took over and she was up in a flash, running flat out with Flint and Max hanging on for dear life. *UUUURRRRRR.* She dodged bushes in a zigzag course, desperately looking for a tree to climb. *UUUURRRRRR.* But the branches were too high. Spotting a giant mahogany tree ahead, she raced for it, ignoring the thorns ripping her legs. She hunkered down behind the tree only to find that Pinky and Perky were already there!

Amazingly, Flint and Max were still riveted to her, too terrified to make a noise.

RUFF RUFF RUFF RUFF. She heard Bulu in the distance. *RUFF RUFF RUFF RUFF.* He was frantic. Then the shrill blasts of sound like a hundred trumpets. *UUUURRRRRRR UUUURRRRRRR UUUURRRRRR.* The blares of the elephant were paralyzing. Anna listened for Bulu. His bark could barely be heard above the trumpeting. Gradually, the elephant's screams began to diminish, becoming fainter and fainter. Then all was eerily quiet. There was no further sound from Bulu.

For what seemed an eternity, Anna remained frozen behind the tree, heart pounding, ignoring the buzzing and biting of tsetse flies. She was listening. Wondering if the elephant was looking for her. Trying to get her bearings, she peeked around the tree. All appeared clear.

She slowly began to pick her way through the brush back to the road. The bike lay on its side. She cautiously peered around, the silence loud in her ears. There was no sign of the elephant. Or Bulu.

Flint made a little whimper. Bulu was trotting down the road! "Thank God," Anna said in a breathless whisper. He was still growling in distress. He turned around to look behind him and gave a little bark. When he walked up to her, Anna knelt down to hug him. He was trembling. So was she. So much so that she couldn't pick up the bike and just sat, instead, on the edge of the road. She felt that if the elephant returned, she might not have the stamina to escape.

For several minutes, Anna took long, deep breaths. Pinky and Perky stood by quietly, looking as though nothing had happened. She watched Bulu for a moment. She knew that if the elephant had not been so confounded by the bold little dog, she could have been killed. She got to her feet, picked up the bike, and glanced nervously around. No sign or sound of the elephant. She got back on the seat and pedaled toward home.

A week later, Anna stood in the doorway of the bush house watching the sun come up over the hills. She was waiting for ZAWA to arrive. Bulu heard the engine first and raced out the door and down the driveway. The truck was on time. She and Steve had requested that they arrive at dawn so that Jack, Flint, and Max would still be asleep in their cages. Steve walked out of the house and put his arm around Anna. They saw the Land Rover appear between the trees.

"I guess it's time to bring them out," Steve said as he

squeezed Anna's arm. Walking back inside, he looked over at the monkeys' crates against the wall. He was grateful they were asleep. If they could remain slumbering, he might be able to transfer them to the truck before they awakened.

The Land Rover rumbled up to the doorway as Anna stepped forward. A ZAWA ranger climbed out and snapped a salute. "Miss Anna. I come to take monkeys." Anna nodded. "Thank you," she said, trying to remain casual, as though he were picking up a package.

Steve appeared at the door holding the cage that contained Flint and Mad Max. The ranger turned and swung open the truck's rear door. Steve quietly slid the crate onto the floor, its wire door facing out the back. He returned to the house and in a moment came back out carrying Jack's cage. He slipped it slowly on the floorboard so that it also faced outward. Bulu appeared at Steve's feet, his eyes fixed on the monkeys. This was not the usual morning routine.

Bulu stood up on his hind feet, trying to look in the back of the truck. He started to whine. Anna stood quietly by the door watching Bulu. He seldom if ever made whining noises unless physically distressed. Did he know that the monkeys were leaving for good? Bulu barked once, a short chuffing sound.

Jack suddenly woke up, his eyes shifting back and forth as he tried to comprehend his surroundings. He pushed his face to the wire and whimpered, waking Flint and Max. Their eyes shot open and their fingers began to intertwine the wire. They pressed their faces tight against the wire, trying to see downward where Bulu was whining. Then they spotted Anna by the doorway and Steve standing to the right of the open truck door. It registered that their cages were not in the house. They had been placed in a peculiar place with strange smells. *Eeeeeeee eeeeeeee eeeeeeee.* Flint's and Max's eyes turned wild in confusion. *Eeeeeeee eeeeeeee eeeeeeee.* Jack called to Flint and Max. Anna stood still, her face set, her emotions in check.

"All right, guys," Steve said, keeping his voice steady. "It's going to be okay." The ranger held the back door open until Steve gave the word to shut it. Flint and Max whimpered again, waiting for Steve and Anna to open their cages like they did every morning. Jack turned peculiarly quiet, poking his fingers through the wire, trying to reach out for Steve. "You'll be all right, Jack," Steve said, holding himself back, resisting every urge to put his hand out to touch him. "Just think, you'll probably have a girlfriend soon." Jack tried to stretch his fingers farther forward to touch Steve.

Bulu remained standing up against the Land Rover's rear door. Steve picked him up and held him in the crook of his arm. Bulu wagged his tail when he saw his friends. "You'll be free," Steve said. "Probably have families of your own one of these days." Then he nodded to the ranger to close the door. But before he could, Steve put his free hand up. The ranger hesitated. Steve moved forward and reached out to touch Jack's fingers. His face stony, Steve lingered a moment, then nodded to the ranger, who walked forward and slowly closed the truck door. Bulu jumped from Steve's arm to the ground. Steve stood beside Anna, who had both hands over her mouth. The ranger saluted, then climbed behind the wheel. As the truck began to drive away, Bulu glanced at Steve and Anna, confused. When the truck approached the end of the driveway, Bulu suddenly started to run after it. But he soon halted and turned to look at Steve and Anna. As the ranger drove onto the road, Bulu sat down. He watched the truck as it disappeared into the bush and was gone.

Each morning for the next few days, Bulu walked to the end of the driveway to look down the road. He continued his vigil, waiting for the truck. But it never returned. Then, about a week later, Bulu no longer watched for it. He finally seemed to accept that Jack, Flint, and Max would not be coming back.

At every opportunity, however, Bulu still trotted off into the bush with Pinky and Perky. But they had been losing interest in the dog's chase games. They had their minds focused on other things, like looking for boyfriends. When the warthogs stopped to forage for roots under shady tree groves, they continually stirred up clouds of tsetses. The maddening flies also swarmed around Bulu, driving him to distraction with their painful bites. His enthusiasm for straying off with the warthogs was waning.

One afternoon about a week later, Bulu walked through the door of the center. He stopped and panted, his head hanging down heavily. Then he moved toward his water bowl. He wanted to drink, but he turned his mouth away. With great effort, he lay down slowly behind a display case. Steve and Anna were standing on ladders placing snares on the wall for the anti-poaching display. Distracted by their work, they hadn't seen Bulu enter the room. They were focused on putting the final touches on the exhibits for the grand opening of the wildlife education facility. In approximately three weeks, they would drive to the Chitimandu village school to bring thirty-six students and their headmaster to the center.

A half hour later, Anna stepped down from the ladder and glanced around the room at the exhibits. She and Steve had organized each one to teach children how communities used, or abused, a natural resource—water, trees, soil, wildlife. They also wanted to give the students a sense of the valley's history. One display held ancient stone weapons, flint tools, and fossils found in the area. But the primary purpose of the center was to show how to conserve Luangwa's fragile resources and wild animals.

As Anna walked past a display case, she did a double take. Bulu's tail was sticking out from behind it. "Well, Bulu," she said, "all tuckered out today?" She didn't notice that Bulu hadn't touched his water bowl. She walked back to the anti-poaching display area. It was the final section she and Steve were preparing. She looked at the large white object on a table. A rhino skull. Cracked and bleached from the sun, it was missing its horn, which had been poached decades earlier. As Anna stared at the skull, an empty feeling came over her. What was it like for the very last living rhino in the valley? Did it die of despair not finding another of its species? As Anna concentrated on the skull, she had an inspiration. "Steve," she said, looking up at him on the ladder. "Remember when Chief Kakumbi told us about the *chipembele* that stumbled into the wedding feast—"

"—and kicked over the village beer pot!" Steve laughed. "Imagine a rhino crashing a party."

"I have an idea," Anna said as Steve stepped down from the ladder. "You know how we've been thinking of what to call the center?" She looked at the rhino skull. "Why don't we christen it . . . the Chipembele Wildlife Education Center?"

Steve thought a moment as he studied the skull. He placed his hand on it. "Yes. So the children *see* that nothing like this ever happens again."

It was late afternoon when they finished the anti-poaching display. "I'm starved," Steve said, folding up a stepladder.

"Beans on toast?" Anna smiled at him.

"Sounds heavenly." Steve chuckled.

As Anna headed toward the door, she passed the glass case where Bulu had lain down. His tail was still sticking out from behind it. "Hey, Mister Sleepyhead," she called. "Let's head for home. Time for supper."

But Bulu didn't move, not even his tail. Then she noticed that his water dish hadn't been touched. He always lapped it dry. Alarmed, she got to her knees to look behind the case. She placed her hand on his back, but he didn't stir. "Steve! There's something wrong with Bulu!"

Steve rushed over, pulled the case aside, knelt down beside Anna, and put his hand on Bulu's chest. He looked worried. "His heart's racing like crazy." Then he felt Bulu's head. "He's burning up. A fever."

"I'll get the thermometer." Anna raced out the door. Moments later, she returned. When they took Bulu's temperature, they were shocked to see that it was 106 degrees! Three and a half degrees above the normal 102.5 for a dog. Steve gently picked Bulu up to carry him back to the house. "Let's give him some aspirin to try to lower the fever."

Anna stood at the table grinding aspirin into a powder. Bulu lay on a blanket on the table. As Steve placed a cool, damp towel over him, he suddenly remembered something. Mitch's words of warning. *Extremely high temperature . . . when a* terrier *has no energy . . . something's wrong.* "Anna. I think Bulu's got the tryps."

She looked at him, alarmed. Then she thought a moment. "The *tsetses!*"

Steve nodded. "How could I be so *stupid*?" He shot his hands up. "Mitch even *warned* me about the symptoms."

They both felt guilty. Having been so focused on their work, they'd misread Bulu's first signs of the disease—believing his sluggishness was from the ever-soaring temperatures of the dry season. They too had been dragging their tail feathers in the blasting heat.

"Berenil," Steve said, recalling what Mitch told him. "It's a medicine. Mitch told me that it's used for sleeping sickness."

"Is it a *cure*?"

"It can be." Steve put his hand on Anna's shoulder. "Look. I'll level with you. Mitch warned me that berenil's a poison that—"

"A *poison*?"

"A poison that kills the tryps parasite. It's injected to protect cattle. But the dosage for small animals is very dicey." He put his hand on Bulu.

"Which means the cure could kill him?"

Steve nodded. "But without berenil, he has no chance at all."

"Then we've got to get him to Lusaka!" Anna said. "I'm sure our vet will have it."

"In his weakened condition, he'd never survive a flight to Lusaka." Steve thought a moment. "Mitch told me there's a veterinary clinic in Chipata. He cautioned that it's not much of an animal hospital. But it's our only choice." He looked to the doorway and noticed the fading light of the afternoon. "We must get him there now." Steve stood up, thinking. "I'll have Mabvuto drive you to Chipata. With poachers about, I need to stay here to watch the fort."

Wrapped in a blanket in the backseat, Bulu remained asleep as the Land Rover lurched along the rough road to Chipata. Anna sat beside him. The sun settled behind the cliffs of the escarpment. Mabvuto switched on the headlights to maneuver slowly around potholes like small craters. Anna gazed out the window and saw sparks of light beginning to pierce the blackness.

All throughout the valley, village people were starting their fires for the night. The evening ritual punctuated the timeless connection of African families to nature. It made Anna recall reading about the famed Scottish explorer Dr. David Livingstone, who trekked through the Luangwa Valley in 1866. He wrote, "It is impossible to describe its luxuriance." Anna was charmed that Livingstone had walked the valley with a little poodle he named Chitane, "the spirited one." He wrote that his fearless dog "had more spunk than a hundred country dogs." One day, Chitane ventured too far into a woodland swamp and was never seen again. Probably drowned or taken by a crocodile. Anna looked down at Bulu and stroked him. He stirred a little bit as though wanting to get up. "Mabvuto, could we stop?"

The Land Rover pulled off to the side of the road.

Mabvuto helped Anna lift Bulu gingerly from the seat. They put him on the ground in front of the headlights. Bulu could barely walk on wobbling legs. Thinking that he only needed to pee, they were horrified when they saw him stop and vomit—*blood!* A dark pool stained the dusty ground. Anna grabbed him and got back in the truck. "Mabvuto," she said, holding Bulu tight. "Can we drive any faster?"

Mabvuto looked at the crumbling road ahead in the glare of the headlights. "I try, Miss Anna. I try."

The sun had just risen above the Malawi hills as Mabvuto drove into Chipata. The border town is a hodgepodge of African markets and old colonial-style stores with porches and tin roofs along a tree-lined street. Shopkeepers were busy unlocking the security gates of their businesses. In the truck's backseat, Anna kept her hand on Bulu's chest. His heartbeat was slow and he was sleeping deeply, as though in a coma.

Mabvuto spotted a side alley with a sign pointing to the veterinary clinic. A moment later, they pulled up in front of a dingy gray building, pockmarked with flaking paint. Anna was relieved to see the door was open. She cradled Bulu in her arms as Mabvuto led the way up the cement steps. Walking in the entryway, she was shocked. Mitch's remark that it wasn't much of a hospital was an understatement! No partition divided the surgery area from the front office. Dried blood was splattered on the walls, and dirty gauze bandages were scattered about the "operating room." Used hypodermic needles were carelessly stuck into murky jars. There was one person there, a man sitting behind a reception desk pouring tea from a large pot. Frantic, Anna rushed up to him. "Where's the doctor?" she demanded.

"He not here," the man answered, barely looking up from his tea.

"Then find him!" she hissed.

"He in Lusaka," he stated flatly, adding sugar to his cup.

"Lusaka?" Anna could barely control her panic. "Our dog. He's got the tryps. He needs berenil!"

"What berenil?" the man asked.

"It's *medicine*," she practically yelled. "Don't you understand? *Please.*" She glanced at Bulu in her arms and started to cry. "He's going to die without it." Desperately, she looked around her. "Oh, Mabvuto. What are we going to do?"

Mabvuto walked directly up to the desk. "Sir. Maybe

some other person we talk to? Someone who know about medicine?"

The man slowly stirred his tea. "You can talk to assistant. He come soon."

"*Assistant?*" Anna asked hopefully.

"Yes. He here when doctor gone." He gestured with his teaspoon to a broken-down plastic couch. "You wait there."

A half hour later, a young man in a white coat walked through the door. Anna gently handed Bulu over to Mabvuto and got to her feet. "Sir. Are you the doctor's assistant?"

He nodded, then noticed Mabvuto cradling the dog. "What is the matter?"

"Our dog is very, very sick. I think he has the tryps. He needs a medicine called—"

"—berenil," the assistant interrupted.

"Do you have it?"

The assistant walked over to the medicine storage cabinet. He riffled through some packages for a few moments. "Ah!" He pulled out a packet and held it up. "Yes, we have."

"Thank God!" Anna grabbed Mabvuto's shoulder. She turned back to the doctor. "You can give him the injection now?"

"We must do blood test first," the assistant said as he reached for a hypodermic in one of the cloudy jars.

Anna immediately stepped forward. "Do you mind if we add some more antiseptic? Just as a precaution."

The assistant nodded and carefully cleaned the needles. Then he motioned to Mabvuto to bring the dog.

Bulu lay listless on his side on the examination table. The assistant found a vein on Bulu's left leg and inserted the needle. When he finished drawing the blood, he walked toward a small room. "I am going to the lab. It will take time to examine."

A while later, he returned, shaking his head. "Not good. Microscope show high density of parasites. They can travel to the fluid in brain. Very bad case of tryps."

Anna started to tremble. "The berenil. It will take care of this? Yes?"

The assistant looked down at Bulu on the table. "He very small. I can only inject a little because—"

"—it's poison," Anna interrupted. "I know. I've been warned." She put her hand on Bulu. Then she nodded for the man to proceed.

The assistant opened the packet of berenil and prepared the hypodermic. He found the vein on Bulu's leg and inserted the needle. His thumb slowly pushed the serum through the syringe. When done, he noticed

Anna's alarmed expression. "Madam. I once give injection of berenil to a small dog before."

"Only *once* before?" Anna raised her eyebrows.

"Yes." He smiled at her. "And the dog. He live."

A short while later, the Land Rover left the outskirts of Chipata for home. In the backseat, Anna kept her vigil monitoring Bulu's heartbeat. Slow, but steady. She was encouraged when he opened his eyes. She put a medicine dropper of water to his lips and he drank, a dribble at a time. She looked ahead at the long, dusty, rough road. It would be well after dark before they got back.

That night, Steve and Anna took turns nursing Bulu every two hours. They knew the odds were not in his favor because of the advanced stage of the infection. But they would do everything they could, primarily keeping him hydrated. They carried him outside and laid him on the cool sand and covered him with wet towels to try to bring down his fever.

During the next couple of days, they saw hope. Even though Bulu had lost a lot of weight, he started to gain an appetite. He began to drink milk and nibble mashed eggs, fish, and cheese. Slowly, Bulu appeared to be recovering.

One morning, there was a turning point. Bulu got to his feet. He sniffed the air and looked to the river. In the succeeding days, he was able to walk short distances.

A week later, Bulu had regained his full strength. To be safe, Steve and Anna decided to fly him to Lusaka to be tested by their veterinarian. Anna would accompany Bulu on the plane. At the Lusaka clinic, the vet gave him a thorough physical exam. She was pleased to see his remarkable recuperation and gave him a clean bill of health. As a precaution, she provided Anna with a supply of berenil and instructed her how to inject the correct dosage. There was no doubt that Bulu would be infected again by tsetses.

With Bulu now fully recovered, Steve and Anna could focus totally on the opening of the center. In two days' time, they would drive to the remote Chitimandu village school. A tourist lodge was providing an open-back truck and a driver to bus thirty-six children to the center.

21

RUFF RUFF RUFF RUFF. Bulu went nuts when he saw the rooster strutting across the road. He climbed halfway out the driver's window barking in outrage. *RUFF RUFF RUFF RUFF*. The rooster swaggered, his neck moving in rhythm to his feet. "Who's king of the road *now*, Mister Bulu?" Steve chuckled as the rooster ignored the Land Rover and took his own sweet time. Then Bulu spotted a village scavenger dog skulking around a cluster of thatched huts. Bulu rarely saw other dogs. He jumped across Anna's lap and leaned out her window to growl. Steve and Anna were on their way to Chitimandu school. Once there, they would connect with the lodge truck to transport the students to Chipembele's grand opening.

"I wonder how the youngsters will react to Bulu?" Anna asked, resting her cheek against Bulu's back. "You know, he's never been around any children."

"And these kids have never been around any *pet* dogs. We'll soon find out." He pointed to the CHITIMANDU

SCHOOL sign beside the road. He turned the Land Rover into a wide, sandy courtyard and headed for a long cement building with a red tin roof. A group of thirty-six giggling girls and boys, ages seven to fourteen, stood in front of the school, dressed in green uniform shorts and skirts. They were not wearing shoes.

The open-back truck had already arrived, parked under a lone mango tree surrounded by clumps of tree stumps. Most of them had been cut down for cooking fires and charcoal. A green and gold Zambian flag stirred nearby on a tall pole as dust tornadoes whirled around its base. When Steve and Anna stepped from the Land Rover, the children started to clap. Mr. Bandala, a short bald man in a blue cotton shirt and slacks, waddled out of the headmaster's office. "Mister Steve! Miss Anna!" He did a little bow and grabbed their hands. "Welcome. Welcome. The children. They tell me they not sleep for *two* nights. They very excited." When he looked back at his students, he saw they had suddenly turned mute. They were now fixated on something in the Land Rover. A small figure had its forepaws up on the steering wheel to see better, its pointed face staring at them through the windshield. Bulu was silent, studying the children, absolutely fascinated, his tail wagging furiously.

"Oh, Mr. Bandala," Anna said. "That's our dog, Bulu. He's really quite harm—" And just then Bulu jumped out the driver's window and ran directly for the kids. The smaller ones shrieked and huddled together. Bulu stopped. *Ruff ruff ruff.* He was confused by their terrified screams, his tail now rigid. "Bulu! *Bulu!*" Anna rushed over to put her arms around him. "It's all right, boys and girls. Bulu won't hurt you. He's just curious." *Ruff ruff ruff.* The littlest kids started to cry as their older brothers and sisters comforted them.

"It *okay*. Dog *okay*." Mr. Bandala toddled over to the kids like a father goose to hug them. "Oh, sorry, Miss Anna. Mister Steve. I apologize much," he said. "They frightened because the dogs in the village sometimes bite." He looked at the Land Rover and laughed. "And the smallest children, they think your dog can *drive* truck."

Steve had an idea as he watched the kids' fearful reaction. "Mr. Bandala," he said, putting his hand on the headmaster's shoulder. "Do you have a ball I could borrow for a moment?"

"Yes," Mr. Bandala replied, looking a bit puzzled.

"Could you get it for me?"

Mr. Bandala turned and disappeared into his office. While he was gone, Anna stepped up onto the porch to peer into a classroom. It was almost barren, with just a few benches for desks and a broken blackboard. A torn world map hung on the wall, and there was one shelf of old textbooks. Anna quickly made mental notes of what the students needed.

Mr. Bandala walked back out of his office. He held a round wad of leather, stitched together in pieces. Noticing Steve's perplexed gaze, Mr. Bandala was somewhat embarrassed. "I sorry," he said, handing over the object. "The best we have."

Steve then realized he was holding a small *homemade* soccer ball. The school could not afford a real one. Steve smiled at Mr. Bandala, marveling at his ingenuity. "This is perfect, Mr. Bandala. I will replace it."

Steve looked over at Bulu, still staring at the children. "Bulu! Come here, Bulu!" Bulu shot a glance sideways to Steve, then looked warily back at the cluster of kids. "Bulu, come! Let's play!" Steve held up the ball. In a flash, Bulu was at Steve's feet, dancing around like a prizefighter in anticipation. Steve slowly wound up a pitch and let the ball go. Bulu practically flew across the courtyard as the ball traced the sky in an arc. He halted as he tracked the ball's downward curve, jumped at it in midair, and sank his teeth into it like a lion. Then he ran back with it to Steve, who pitched the ball again. Bulu tore up the turf to catch it. But instead of racing back with the ball, he started growling and shaking it until it fell to pieces. Having now killed the ball, Bulu started tearing around the school yard, launching into a crazy spell. Round and round and round he went, eyes wild, barking and barking. "GO, BULU. GO!" Steve and Anna started cheering, clapping, stomping their feet. Bulu was racing about like the White Rabbit, stirring up brown clouds behind him.

Then something strange happened. The children let go of each other's hands. With their eyes wide and mouths hanging open, they started to walk closer to Bulu. They were astonished. This dog not only rode in cars, he knew how to play ball and how to race. They'd never seen such a thing!

"GO, BULU. GO!" Steve and Anna kept up the momentum of the cheers. "GO, BULU. GO!" Then Mr. Bandala joined in, shyly and softly at first. "Go, Bulu. Go!" He started clapping in rhythm and threw off his inhibitions. "GO, BULU. GO! GO, BULU. GO!" The children were now shrieking with laughter. Seeing their headmaster cheering on the dog, the kids joined in. "GO, BULU. GO!" Soon the whole crowd was clapping, stomping, chanting over and over. "GO, BULU. GO! GO, BULU, GO! GO, BULU, GO!"

Thrilled to be the center of attention, Bulu took full advantage. He got crazier and crazier the more the children called his name. He was now running like a greyhound on steroids.

"Bulu sure knows how to work a crowd!" Steve laughed with Anna.

But even Bulu had his limits. After a while, he began to slow down. His tongue hung from his mouth. Then he plopped down under the mango tree, totally exhausted.

The kids applauded. Mr. Bandala's eyes were leaking tears of laughter. He caught his breath and put his hands on Steve's and Anna's shoulders. "The children. They tell about this when they go home," he said. "The elders. I think they not believe them."

A few minutes later, Mr. Bandala herded the children toward the tourist truck. They climbed the ladder to take their seats in the open-back vehicle. As Anna stood nearby, she had a chance to observe them up close. Their uniforms were frayed and threadbare. She added the observation to her mental notes about the kids' needs. In about five weeks, she planned to fly to England to buy supplies for the wildlife center.

When all his students were on board, Mr. Bandala

took a seat in the front. The lodge driver started the engine and slammed it into gear. Just as the tourist truck rumbled across the courtyard, the children exploded into a cheer as though they were on a rocket to the moon. It brought tears to Anna's eyes. She thought how special these Zambian children were. Shy, unspoiled—and so excited that they hadn't slept for two nights in anticipation of the natural wonders they might see. So free from the trap of material things that ensnares the kids of the Western world.

As the open-back truck rounded a curve, six giraffes suddenly loomed above the road. The herd was thirty feet ahead and towered above the vehicle. The students instantly got to their feet. They'd never seen giraffes before! Although the children had witnessed elephants raiding their gardens, the shy giraffes never ventured near the villages. Steve and Anna slowly rolled the Land Rover up beside the tourist truck and cut the engine. "What a stroke of luck, hey?" Steve whispered to Anna. The kids were awestruck, not one of them making a sound. Then the peaceful scene was shattered. *Grrrrrrrrr.* Bulu stuck his head out the window. *RUFF RUFF RUFF RUFF.* One of the giraffes shifted a foot, uneasy about the noise, then moved across the road as his companions paced behind in single file. The children burst out in laughter. They were astonished that the little white dog could order giraffes off the road.

Ummmph ummmph ummmph. Hippos grunted as the crowd of students lined the riverbank beside the gazebo. The kids were spellbound by the animals and the beauty of the unspoiled woodlands. Most villagers never travel more than a few miles from home. Bicycles are their

only way around. As a result, the Luangwa and its wildlife remain a mystery to local people living in remote communities.

"Welcome to the grand opening of the Chipembele Wildlife Education Center," Anna announced proudly as she stood beside Steve on the bank. "Today you'll be touring the center and doing a bush walk along the river."

"You'll see all kinds of wild animals," Steve added. The youngsters grabbed each other's hands in excitement. "Now, everyone must stay in single file behind me. Mr. Bandala will be at the rear. And please stay quiet. We don't want to scare anything away." He unshouldered his .458 Winchester. "Okay, we're ready to move."

One twelve-year-old boy had his eyes fixed on the rifle. "Sir," he said. "Are you going to shoot the animals?"

"No," Steve answered. "This rifle is for protection. Most wild animals are more afraid of us than we are of them." He pointed at the river. "But there are a few exceptions such as—" *Ruff ruff ruff.* The kids' heads turned as one in alarm. Bulu was running with two strange-looking wild animals, heading straight toward the crowd! The littlest kids burst into tears.

"It's okay, boys and girls!" Steve put his hands up for

calm. Then he put down his gun. "It's only Pinky and Perky. They're *warthogs.* Bulu's *friends.*" Having never seen a warthog before, the small children banded together as the older ones froze.

"They're *fat,*" a girl said as she clutched her little brother.

"They're *pregnant,*" Anna informed her. "They'll be having babies soon."

Seeing that the youngsters were still intimidated, Steve thought of something. "Pinky! Perky!" he called, and clapped. "It's beauty treatment time!" The warthogs trotted over as he held out his hand. Then they lay on the ground. Steve knelt down and vigorously scratched their hides. Pinky and Perky slowly rolled their eyes into the backs of their heads. The children's mouths were hanging open. They were absolutely mesmerized.

"Come on over, kids," Anna urged. "You can help groom Pinky and Perky." She walked up to Bulu. "And Mister Bulu will introduce you to them."

"Go on, children," Mr. Bandala encouraged.

Gradually, one by one, each girl and boy came forward. Bulu cocked his head at the kids, then slowly walked toward them. He stopped beside two of the smallest ones. They found their courage, reached out, and put their hands on Bulu. His tail immediately started to wag. Seeing that, the rest of the kids moved forward to pet him. Then all the boys and girls were jostling for space to put their hands on the small white dog. "Bulu. Ohh, Bulu. *Ohhhh, Buuluu.*" They were cooing his name. Bulu's tail was a blur. His lips stretched over his teeth in a grin.

Steve got up to stand beside Anna. They watched the children, who were charmed. For the first time ever, these kids touched an animal with *affection.*

Then the youngsters walked over to look at the warthogs up close. Soon Pinky and Perky had hundreds of fingers rubbing, scratching, and tickling their hides. The music of the children's laughter carried far across the river.

⌒

Anna prepared lunch for the children while Steve was guiding the bush walk. At noon, she stepped outside the gazebo to help Mabvuto arrange benches under the trees. "Do you think we'll have enough food?" she asked.

Mabvuto looked toward the gazebo. Tables were laden with covered dishes of fish, rice, cassava, and potatoes, pitchers of milk, thermoses of orange squash, pots of tea, and baskets of bread and cookies. "Did you invite the hippos too?" He laughed.

A short while later, Anna saw Steve step onto the embankment with the children. Mr. Bandala was behind them. Two little girls, about twelve years old, were holding Steve's hands. Anna smiled. It looked as though Steve had become a father figure, or hero, to them. *But of course,* she thought. Many of the kids had lost a father or mother to the disease of AIDS. Thousands of children in Zambia are left orphaned every year by the spread of HIV.

"I want to be wildlife ranger," announced one of the girls to Anna and Mabvuto. "Me too!" the other girl piped up. "To guard animals."

Steve winked at Anna. "It was a great bush walk. I'd like you to meet my new friends Thandiwe and Emily. They asked about everything along the river—plants, birds, insects."

"Well, we may have some future rangers, huh?" Anna smiled at them.

Steve put his hands on the girls' shoulders. "I bet when you grow up, you'll be the chief wildlife wardens of South Luangwa National Park. If you study hard."

Bulu trotted up the bank beside a little boy, who raced over to Anna. "Bulu. He run everywhere!" he blurted out. "He brave. No afraid nothing."

"Hmmm, maybe just some things. He's not fond of crocs or hippos." She smiled at the boy. "And what's your name?"

"Joseph. I seven," he said "Can I adopt Bulu?"

"He's already taken," Anna chuckled, putting her hand on the boy's head. "Now let's go have lunch." She stepped into the gazebo and saw the children had suddenly turned quiet, their eyes riveted to the tables. Mabvuto was uncovering the dishes, the pots, and the bread baskets. The kids put their hands to their mouths in amazement. Then they applauded.

Mr. Bandala rushed into the gazebo, clasping his hands, bowing slightly. "Thank you, Miss Anna. The children so happy. They eat mostly cornmeal, millet, vegetables, and fruit each day." He looked around at the tables. "But here, they *never* see so many kinds of food."

❧

Click click click click. The sharp hooves of Pinky and Perky tapped along the cement floor as they followed the kids into the center. "Out! Out!" Anna ordered

Pinky and Perky, giving them a playful slap on their hides. "This isn't the Warthog Academy." The children laughed as Pinky and Perky turned and clicked their way outside. Then Bulu walked in with Joseph at his side. The boy continued to fuss over Bulu, talking to him and petting him.

For the next two hours, Anna and Steve presented lessons about conserving the biodiversity of Luangwa's natural resources. They began their instruction at the forest preservation exhibit. The older children opened pocket-sized notebooks to write in English, the official language of Zambia. A three-dimensional display showed a tree sapling in a large pot cut in half. Steve dug into the dirt to expose roots that held the soil and water. The children could see how a tree prevents erosion.

Anna demonstrated the correct way to cut limbs for firewood without killing the tree and how to plant saplings. She gave a short lecture on the disastrous effects of the unregulated charcoal business. Photos taken in Luangwa showed illegal charcoal kilns. The ovens burned tree after tree, reducing forests to scrubland. The businesses never replanted. The waste of wood astounded the students. A hands-on exhibit offered lessons for net fishing. A wire mannequin fisherman sat in a real dugout canoe. The children held and examined two types of netting. One was the illegal, small-hole mesh pattern that trapped all fish, even the tiny babies. But the larger-hole mesh, the lawful one, was designed to allow smaller fish to escape for future breeding.

"And here's the animal poop display," Steve announced as the students laughed. He pointed to twenty baskets on a table containing the dried dung of various wildlife species. The exhibit's purpose was to show how everything gets recycled in the bush. "You can usually tell whether an animal is a vegetarian or a carnivore," Steve informed them, "by examining its waste." He pointed to a hyena's droppings. "It's white because of calcium. A hyena's powerful jaws grind up bones and hooves. He eats every part of the animal. Notice bits of hide and hair too."

"Eewww." The students made faces and giggled.

"This is hippo excrement," Anna said, holding up a basket. "See how it's broken up into small pieces? The hippo's fat tail paddles like a manure spreader, scattering nutrients into the river to feed the fish."

Steve picked up an elephant dropping the size of a bowling ball. "Strictly vegetarian," he said, pointing out details. "Observe the grass, bark, and lots and lots of seeds." Steve showed a photo of a small sapling growing out of an elephant dropping. "The elephant," he stressed, "is Luangwa's tree planter." Then he held up another elephant dropping, hardened into a perfectly smooth ball with a hole in one side. "This is a *house*. It was rolled smooth into a ball by a dung beetle. The dung beetle lays its eggs inside the ball, then days later, when the eggs hatch, the larvae eat the dung. It's like being born inside a loaf of bread!" The children laughed. "Then countless beetles will enrich the soil. Generation after generation by the millions, repeating the cycle throughout the valley."

Anna stepped forward. "Now you see why every plant and animal is dependent on the other for survival," she informed them. "Biodiversity is like a spider's web. Remove too many strands and Luangwa's ecosystem will fall apart."

Steve and Anna then led them to the anti-poaching exhibit. The children suddenly turned quiet. They focused on a large picture hung beneath wire snares on the wall. The photo showed an emaciated animal who appeared to be wearing a red collar. It was a lioness with a horrific open wound encircling her throat. She was a living skeleton.

"A poacher's snare did this," Anna said. "She was trapped for days without water or food in terrible agony. She was beyond saving. The rangers had to shoot her."

The students put their hands to their mouths in pity. They stared at other gruesome photos. Antelope, zebras, giraffes—all of them caught in wire traps. Steve reached up and took a snare off the wall. "All this poaching is caused by the bush meat trade." He pulled the noose tight on the wire loop. "*It's against the law* to trap wild animals for food."

Anna held up a dried fish. "But here's a lawful and *renewable* source of protein—fish. And it's healthier than meat. Remember"—she smiled—"if you use a legal fishnet, you'll have a source of protein forever."

"What's *that*?" Thandiwe put her hand on a large white bone on a table.

"A skull of a rhinoceros," Anna answered. "A *chipembele* . . . the inspiration for this center." She then pointed to a photo of a mother rhino and her baby. "Every single *chipembele*—some eight thousand of them—was killed in the valley before you were born. The poachers sold off their horns to faraway countries, China, Yemen." She looked directly at the students. "This could happen to *all* of Luangwa's wild animals unless we—"

"—do something to stop it!" Mr. Bandala said. Then he stared hard at his students, searching their faces.

Thandiwe was the first to step forward. "We will

245

study hard, Mr. Bandala. We want to come back to Chipembele to learn more. How to protect our trees, fish—"

"—and *animals*!" Emily said. "You please give us more information, Mister Steve, Miss Anna? Then we teach our village. And other villages."

Finding courage through Emily and Thandiwe, all the shy students began to raise their hands, one after another. "Me too! Me too! Me too!"

Anna and Steve nodded at each other. They knew the children were going to lead the way into the future.

"There an orphan—like me!" Joseph called out as he pointed to another photo. It was a picture of a baby elephant standing beside its dead mother. Poachers had shot her and her face had been chopped off to remove its ivory.

Steve observed the children's shock at the overpowering image. "Girls and boys," he said. "I have something to show you. Please follow Anna and me outside."

A moment later, the kids stood before the foundation of a building in the initial stage of construction. Mabvuto was laying cinder blocks, with the help of two newly hired workers, Busanga and Dixson. "This structure, when finished, will be the first section for the orphanage," Steve said. "It's going to be a—"

"—home for baby animals?" Joseph asked.

"You guessed right. Mainly for elephants," Anna said.

"Bulu and I help you?" Joseph asked as he stroked Bulu beside him.

"Well . . . yes," Steve said. "Bulu's already raised Pinky and Perky and a bushbuck, two vervets, and a baboon."

"I can help make house for orphans," Joseph said. "I build one before."

"Really?" Steve chuckled.

Mr. Bandala spoke up. "*Really*. Joseph's parents die two years ago. His thirteen-year-old brother—the oldest—is now head of family. He watch over his seven little sisters and brothers. Each child help make mud bricks. Together, they *all* build house."

Steve and Anna were astonished as they looked at the little lad.

"Bulu. He big brother to baby animals," Joseph announced, his face beaming. "Bulu make them like family. They be orphans no more."

The sun began to sag over the woodlands as the children walked to the lodge truck. "This *wonderful* day!" Mr.

Bandala said to Steve and Anna, standing beside the vehicle. "It go fast." He looked at the kids climbing the ladder to take their seats. "My students. They learn so much to help wild animals."

"We learned much from them too," Anna said. "About the human spirit."

"The children. They have gift for you before they go," Mr. Bandala said. He signaled to the kids and they stood up. "The song, Mister Steve and Miss Anna. It is about sisterhood and brotherhood. They sing it to you in their tribal language."

The girls' lilting voices started off with soft tones, slowly building in volume. Then the boys' voices harmonized, all the children singing like a church choir and clapping. Steve's and Anna's hearts soared and they too started to clap to the rhythm. They did not need a translator to understand it was about the simple joys of life. "Thank you, thank you." Steve and Anna applauded the children.

"We very grateful to you." Mr. Bandala shook Steve's and Anna's hands.

"I come back?" a small voice asked. Steve and Anna turned around. Joseph had lagged behind. He was on his knees with his arms clasped around Bulu's neck.

"I promise. You will come back to see him," Anna said.

Reassured, Joseph loosened his grip, stood up, and kissed Bulu on the head. Then he scrambled up the ladder to join his classmates.

The students called out their goodbyes as the engine rumbled to life and the truck slowly swayed down the driveway. Excited by the kids' laughter, Bulu started to race after them, barking. The children, watching him running behind, got to their feet. Then, pumping their arms up and down, they chanted a salute. "BUUU-lu BUUU-lu BUUU-lu." At the end of the driveway, Bulu slowed to a trot and stopped as the truck rolled down the road, gaining speed. "BUUU-lu BUUU-lu BUUU-lu." The children disappeared in a swirl of dust, their cheering rhythms fading into the woodlands. "BUUU-lu BUUU-lu BUUU-lu BUUU-lu BUUU-lu . . ."

22

The yellow eye of the full moon gazed through the smoke of the campfire. Steve and Anna sat in chairs drinking coffee on the riverbank as Bulu sat beside them. They were discussing Anna's upcoming trip to England to purchase education supplies. It had been two weeks since Chipembele's opening, and Anna had already hosted three more school tours. Every day, Steve, Mabvuto, Dixson, and Busanga labored in the brutal heat digging postholes for the elephant stockade fence. Ever since ZAWA gave approval to build the orphanage, the work had been nonstop from dawn to dusk.

Bulu started to growl and got to his feet. He was looking downriver. Steve and Anna followed his gaze. About a hundred yards away, walking on the silver sand in the moonlight, was an elephant followed by two smaller ones. There was no mistaking the profile of the leader. One tusk protruding forward, the other straight back, as though twisted in its socket. Steve stood up. "I think it's old Crooked Tooth."

Anna got up and put her hand to her heart. "The elephant Mitch told us about." They had never seen her before, and they were captivated. Crooked Tooth was an older female and rather short in stature for a mature elephant. Mitch told them she had attitude and a withering glare that said, "Go ahead, make my day." She was always in the company of the two smaller elephants. No one knew whether they were offspring, siblings, or orphans that had bonded. But they were inseparable. Sometimes they shadowed larger herds, but always at a distance. Where had the trio come from? It was a mystery.

Bulu always watched elephants intensely. They were the one animal that seemed to enthrall him above all others. It was a fascination that would soon prove to be near fatal.

It all started one morning quite unexpectedly. Steve and the three workers were putting another post into the ground at the stockade. They stopped when they heard the rumbling of an engine. A large truck appeared on the road. Bulu was already trotting down the driveway to greet it. Then suddenly he stopped in his tracks. He held his nose to the air and started sniffing. The musky smell of an animal wafted from a crate in the back. He started to bark frantically and raced after the vehicle.

Anna had heard the truck and walked out of the center. It pulled up to the entryway in a haze of dust. Two rangers from the South Luangwa Conservation Society were standing behind the crate, two ZAWA rangers in front. A tall blond woman in green khakis, the director of the conservation society, climbed out of the driver's seat.

"Rachel!" Anna stepped forward to greet her just as Steve appeared.

"ZAWA sent me," Rachel said, shaking their hands. "Njovu told me you've been sanctioned to build an elephant orphanage." She chuckled. "I've brought one for you."

"An *elephant*?" Steve and Anna looked at each other, then with dismay at the crate in the truck. "*Now?* We've only just started building the shelter and stockade. All we have is a toolshed."

"Any port in the storm." Rachel smiled.

"We don't know much yet about raising elephants," Anna added. "All we've learned is from our correspondence with Daphne Sheldrick, the lady in Kenya who pioneered elephant orphanages forty years ago."

"Then you've got the drop on me," Rachel said. "I

only know how to rescue them from snares." Rachel turned and walked toward the back of the truck. Bulu was already standing there growling. When she pulled down the tailgate, he stretched up to put his forepaws on it, trying to peek into a cage made of wooden slats. One of the rangers pulled the crate door open, and out walked a three-and-a-half-foot-high elephant. "Meet Chudoba!" Rachel announced. "He's a two-and-a-half-year-old weaned bull."

Anna and Steve broke into grins. *RUFF RUFF RUFF.* Bulu voiced his excitement. Chudoba rocked side to side in jerky movements like a clay animation figure. A rubbery trunk flitted about like a live electrical wire.

"Where'd you rescue him?" Anna asked.

"From a village. Some children found him two weeks ago," Rachel said. "He wandered in among their homes one day from the bush. He lay down and wouldn't get up. We think poachers killed his mother. The herd must've panicked, leaving him behind. He was so traumatized I had to drug him before taking him to headquarters. But he finally calmed down after a few days." She gestured to two of the rangers. "Thanks to these men, who never left the calf's side, even sleeping next to him."

Steve slowly reached his hand toward the elephant.

The little bull turned his head slightly to the side. An intelligent eye, brownish violet in color and framed by a white outer ring, studied him for a moment. A long, curling eyelash blinked. Then he extended his trunk. The tip of it opened and closed like a pink sock puppet and rested a moment on Steve's open palm. "Blow in his trunk," Rachel urged. Steve did so. Chudoba put the tip into his mouth like a child sucking his thumb. "I read that an elephant does that to identify your scent," Rachel said. "He'll remember you forever." She reached for a burlap sack. "This is a gift from the children for Chudoba. Because he wouldn't drink, the kids kept him alive with these." She opened the bag, and out fell a pile of yellow mangoes. Just as she grabbed one, Chudoba's trunk plucked the golden orb from her fingers like a magician. *Squish slurp.* It was gone. Rachel laughed. "We named him Chudoba. It means 'something picked from the bush.'"

Grrrrrrrr. Bulu was standing on tiptoe, his nose still poking over the pulled-down tailgate. "Okay." Steve chuckled. "It's time I introduce you two." He leaned over and hoisted Bulu up onto the tailgate. "Easy now, Bulu. Take it easy." Steve held him back. Bulu narrowed his eyes at the young elephant and growled.

Chudoba kept rocking side to side, as if boogying to

a distant tune. Bulu stood still, mesmerized by the elephant that never stopped moving. Chudoba telescoped his trunk forward. Bulu turned his head away. The trunk hovered a moment, brushed Steve's hand, then snaked closer and closer to Bulu's face. *Grrrrrrr.* The trunk flared its nostrils like a double-barreled vacuum hose, whiffing up Bulu's scent. Fascinated, Bulu stretched his head forward. Just before Chudoba pulled back his trunk, the tip of it tweaked Bulu's nose. Instantly, Bulu wagged his whole hindquarters in delirious excitement. The rangers hooted with laughter at the elephant that kissed the little white dog.

A few minutes later, Steve, Anna, and Rachel stood inside the toolshed. It had a tin roof and a three-foot-high stone wall base, topped with chicken wire wrapped around the structure and covering a cross-framed wood door. Mabvuto, Dixson, and Busanga were nearby, cementing a post in the ground. Curious, they stopped their work to watch as one of the rangers backed the truck up. The others unloaded several hundred-pound sacks of fresh fruit and vegetables and carried them inside. Rachel opened one of the bags and laid the contents on the floor of the shed. A plank was lowered from the back of the truck to the ground. When Chudoba spotted the goodies, he eagerly walked down the ramp and into the enclosure. Chudoba hovered his trunk over the variety of produce and selected a ripe banana. Bulu wandered in and began sniffing the young bull all over. Anna ran her fingers over Chudoba's back, feeling the bristly black hairs sticking up like

wires. "I've never touched an elephant before." She was enchanted.

"Chudoba cannot be left alone even for a minute," Rachel insisted. "If he is, he'll think he's being abandoned."

"How long do we keep him?" Anna asked.

"Two weeks. ZAWA's arranged to transport him to an elephant rehabilitation center in western Zambia. He can bond with other orphaned elephants there." As Rachel started to walk toward the truck to leave, she stopped and turned around. "Chudoba can be very frightened at night. When he was lost, we think he saw lions. When he hears them, he becomes paralyzed."

Steve knew lions wouldn't hesitate to attack an unprotected elephant calf. He looked at the shed's flimsy chicken wire. "A few days ago, I spotted two male lions hanging about the Chowo. It's troubling. Bulu sometimes wanders there with the warthogs." He put his hand on Chudoba. "We'll keep an eye on him."

Steve stoked a log in the campfire as Anna arranged sheets on two cots set beside the shed. Bulu stood inside staring up at Chudoba in the lamplight. A shooting star blazed through the sky. "Quick. Make a wish," said Steve. Anna looked up and made a silent wish, then looked over at Bulu in the shed. He was studying the little elephant, head held to one side, as Chudoba continued to rock and gorge on vegetables and fruit. Every so often, the calf reached out his trunk to touch Bulu, whose tail never stopped wagging. Reassured that his little friend stayed close, Chudoba resumed eating. Anna wondered where Chudoba's wild family was. She was glad that Bulu was there to be what little Joseph called the dog—big brother to baby animals.

Steve walked over to Anna and sat down in his safari chair. He looked into the shed. As if somebody had flipped a switch, Chudoba had suddenly stopped rocking. He stood completely still, his trunk held high as though tasting the air. Bulu turned and trotted out of the shed. He faced the Chowo. *Grrrrrrr.*

Steve and Anna stood up and looked toward the trees. Bulu started to stalk from the firelight into the shadows. Anna grabbed him. "NO!" she said. Steve picked up his rifle and clicked off the safety. He reached for the flashlight on the cot and aimed into the darkness. The beam lit up a stark white tangle of thorns. Steve looked for reflecting eyes that would betray a leopard or lion. Nothing. Whatever was out there must have moved off. Steve would check the ground in the morning. Anna put Bulu in the shed and locked the door. He was still charged up and growling. Chudoba moved close to stand beside him.

Steve and Anna returned to their chairs. They would keep vigil throughout the night.

As the sun rose over the hills, Steve walked along a path through the brush carrying his rifle. He kept his eyes sharp. Within minutes, he found them. Lion tracks. There was no mistaking them, embedded deep in the sand. The cats had been watching last night, drawn to the scent of the young elephant or the warthogs in their den. He hunkered down and deciphered two different sets. Certainly the same males he'd seen a few days before. He followed their trail to the Chowo embankment. The lions might have crossed or gone up the Chowo. When he inspected the riverbed, he found that the hard, compacted mud left no trace. Steve hoped they'd moved far off.

At the end of the two weeks, Chudoba had consumed nearly all his food. Steve and Anna would soon need to replenish the fruit and vegetables from the markets. One thing they quickly learned about nurturing a five-hundred-pound baby round the clock, day after day. It was *exhausting*. They needed a break. On the morning of Rachel's expected return, Anna worked at the center while Steve babysat. At noon, she saw two trucks coming up the driveway—Rachel's and ZAWA's. *RUFF RUFF RUFF RUFF.* Bulu went crazy. Something was moving in a crate on the back of ZAWA's Land Rover. Pulling up to the center, Rachel called out, "I'm afraid I'll need your parenting skills again."

Steve, Anna, and Rachel stood by the shed as a ranger backed up her truck. Four men lowered the tailgate and put down the plank. They had come to transport Chudoba to the facility in western Zambia. Steve opened the shed door, and the rangers enticed the calf out with oranges. Bulu followed as Chudoba was led to the truck and guided up the plank. He watched silently as the elephant walked into the crate and the door was shut. Bulu trotted up the board and stood by the cage. He peeked in, and suddenly Chudoba's trunk reached through the slats to touch the little dog.

"Looks like Bulu made a new friend," Rachel said to Steve and Anna. Then she gestured toward the other crate in the back of the ZAWA truck. "But you'd better keep him away from Chamilandu." A few days before, Rachel explained, a ranger in Chamilandu district reported an adult female elephant lying on the ground. Her small baby stood by silently in shock. On closer inspection, the ranger was alarmed to see that the mother had a horrifically swollen, infected leg. An inch-thick towing cable had gouged a foot-deep wound into the elephant's foot. Rachel was called to the scene to dart the elephant with an immobilizing drug. But seeing that the tendons were severed as if with a cleaver, she knew the elephant was beyond saving. The mother had to be put down.

"Back at headquarters, the rescued calf screamed for days afterward," Rachel said. "She charged at everyone—all three hundred fifty pounds of her— knocking down a man. Her cries were heart-wrenching. I had to tranquilize her just to truck her here." Rachel signaled to a ranger to lower the tailgate. "Well, let me introduce you." A man opened the crate door and a gray figure slowly stepped out. Because she'd been tranquilized, the calf did not rock back and forth like Chudoba. She just stood there. "She's about two years old. You'll only need to keep her a week. When she's stabilized, I'll transport her to the facility." Rachel turned to Anna. "You might want to put Bulu in the house. When the drug wears off, Chamilandu could become aggressive."

Anna nodded and headed for the ZAWA truck to get Bulu.

"We brought food," Rachel said. "The elephant facility donated plenty of it." When the rangers unloaded boxes, Steve was startled. Expecting to see vegetables, he stared at countless tins of dehydrated milk, cans of coconut milk, and *quart-sized* baby bottles with nipples. "Chamilandu's not weaned," Rachel said. "You'll be busy. She drinks about one liter every hour and a half." Rachel chuckled. "Don't worry. I've asked a ranger to stay and help."

When Anna reached the truck, she saw Bulu standing next to the cage beside the rangers. The men were watching the dog with intense interest. Chudoba's trunk, sticking out through the slats, was feeling all along Bulu's back and head. Anna wondered, *What is it Bulu has that so affects orphans?*

About an hour later, Chamilandu seemed to be recovering from the effects of the drug. She began to walk slowly around the inside of the shed, checking everything out with her trunk. Before Rachel had returned to headquarters, she'd demonstrated how to mix the correct amount of coconut milk with dehydrated human formula milk. She explained how elephants cannot tolerate the fat in cow's milk. Then she fed the calf.

It was already nearing time for the next feeding.

Anna stood outside the shed arranging the cans and giant baby bottles on a table. She would let the ranger do the feedings for the first few days until the calf got used to the new human scents.

Back at the house, Steve and the ranger were busy pouring fresh water into buckets from a jug. It would be used to mix the milk formula. Rushed and distracted, Steve had left the door slightly ajar. Bulu, frustrated he'd been confined to the house, stood on the bed looking toward the shed. Then he glanced toward the door and saw the crack of light. He jumped down from the bed and slipped outside.

Moments later, Anna stepped away from the table and walked over to the cots. She had started to arrange the bedding when—*UURRRRRR*—Chamilandu started screaming! Anna whirled around, but because of the three-foot-high wall, she could see only the head and back of the calf through the wire. Chamilandu seemed to have gone crazy, racing around inside. Anna rushed over to the shed. When she reached it, she let out a scream. Bulu was inside—and the elephant was attacking him!

Bulu desperately dodged the calf's lowered head as Chamilandu tried to butt him. "BULU! GET OUT! *GET*

OUT!" Anna screamed. She yanked desperately at the door. It jammed against the padlock. Then she noticed a tear in the chicken wire at the base of the door—the opening where Bulu had squeezed his way in. *UUUR-RRRRRR.* The calf caught Bulu off balance and sent him glancing off the wall. Anna knelt down and reached her hands through the hole. "OVER *HERE,* BULU. *COME!*" Bulu was stunned. To her horror, he just *stood there* as the elephant came for him again. This time the calf knocked him to the floor onto his side. Thinking he would surely be crushed to death as the elephant lowered her head again, Anna screamed and screamed. Bulu suddenly scrambled to his feet. "*HERE,* BULU—COME *THIS* WAY!" Seeing Anna, he came to his senses and ran toward the hole in the fence. When he reached it, she pulled him through just as the calf slammed against the wooden cross-frames on the door.

Anna immediately checked him over. Miraculously, he was uninjured. It had happened so fast. She held Bulu tightly as she sat lifeless on the ground. Bulu, knowing that he was now safe, glared back at Chamilandu and started growling. Then, feeling triumphant that he'd survived the attack, he began howling.

"What's wrong with Bulu?" Steve called out as he

and the ranger ran up to her. He was shocked when he saw the hole in the fencing on the door. Then he knew and shook his head.

Anna continued to tremble. Bulu continued to howl.

Mabvuto pulled the truck up to the house at dawn. Steve stepped out the doorway carrying two suitcases. It was time for Anna to leave on her ten-day trip to England. "At least you'll only have Bulu to babysit," Anna chuckled as Bulu followed her out the door. Three days earlier, Rachel had picked up the calf to transport to western Zambia.

"Yes, but you never know what Rachel might bring us while you're gone." He put the luggage in the Land Rover and turned to hug and kiss Anna. Bulu rushed up, sensing her departure. He knew what suitcases were for. Anna knelt down to give him a hug. Then she climbed into her seat. As the truck headed down the driveway, Bulu ran alongside. When it turned, he sat down and watched it recede into the distance.

Five days after Anna's departure, Steve, Mabvuto, Dixson, and Busanga finished cementing the posts in the ground for the stockade. Dixson and Busanga then left on leave to visit their families.

The following morning, Steve and Mabvuto were hammering Cyclone fencing onto a post when they heard faint barking in the distance. They stopped to listen. It sounded like the sharp alarm call of a baboon. At first they didn't think much of it. A troop of them had been seen at dawn walking along the dry riverbed. When Steve and Mabvuto resumed their work, the barking started again. This time it sounded higher-pitched, almost frantic. Then there was a distant roar. Steve turned his head. "Lions!" he said, putting his hand up. "They're spooking baboons." Mabvuto cocked his head toward the river and nodded. They listened for a few more moments. Silence. Then all seemed okay. They resumed pounding nails.

A few minutes later, Pinky and Perky came bursting

through the brush, running up to the stockade. Something had spooked them. They were alone. "Have you seen Bulu?" Steve asked Mabvuto.

"I see him on river with warthogs. Maybe one hour past," he answered.

Fear stabbed Steve's heart like an ice pick. Maybe the frantic barking they'd heard earlier *wasn't* a baboon. He dropped his hammer and ran to the river as Mabvuto raced behind him. At the embankment, Steve cupped his hands to his mouth. "BULU! BULU!" There was no response. "BULU! *BULU!*" he shouted over and over. Steve hurried down to the riverbed. He examined the ground like a forensic detective. No sign of dog prints. Perhaps Bulu had stuck to the brush along the bank, headed toward the Chowo? It would be easier to track there in the sandy ground. He climbed the embankment to investigate.

He walked slowly along a thorny pathway, his eyes scanning the sand. Several minutes later, he reached another path that led toward the Chowo. Then he spotted them—Bulu's footprints! They crisscrossed those of the warthogs. Steve dropped to the ground. The tracks definitely headed toward the Chowo riverbank. Steve got up and hurried along the trail for another few minutes. Then a jolt. Lion prints. And they *overlapped* Bulu's tracks. The big cats had been *stalking* the dog and warthogs. Steve turned on his heel and raced back along the trail. "Mabvuto!" he shouted as he reached open ground where Mabvuto was standing. "We've got to find Bulu. *Fast!* I'm going for the gun."

Inside the house, Steve grabbed his Winchester from the wall rack and opened the ammunition case. Frantically, he slammed soft-nosed cartridges into the rifle chamber and stuffed extras into his pockets. He filled two canteens and grabbed the binocs. Clutching his gun, he raced outside. "Mabvuto! Stick close to me." They strode across the stubbly grass. Steve clicked off the rifle's safety as they entered the sandy path.

Several minutes later, they reached the spot where Steve had found the lion prints. They followed them to the Chowo bank. But the tracks disappeared at the hard-baked earth of the dried-up riverbed. Standing silently, Steve watched for any movement in the brush across the Chowo. Then he and Mabvuto walked down the embankment. The hardened mud, like cement, showed only old prints. Steve took the canteens from his belt and tried to put the puzzle together. "Mabvuto," he said, sharing a drink. "The lions were certainly after the warthogs. But I think Bulu got in the way."

"Maybe Bulu *stand* in the way," Mabvuto said. "He try to protect warthogs?"

Steve nodded. It was a chilling thought. He picked up his binocs. For several moments, he scanned the banks of the Luangwa. He concentrated on the brush lining the embankment downstream. Then he turned his search onto the bend in the river. When he focused the lenses, something caught his eye. The back ends of two tawny figures. They were loping along about two thousand yards ahead. "*Lions.* Mabvuto! Let's go!"

They quickly rushed down onto the Luangwa streambed. Steve stopped every few moments to look through the binocs. Five minutes or so later, they reached the bend and walked around the curve. They stared down the widening riverbed. The lions had disappeared. Had the cats noticed that two humans were following them, triggering them to pace faster downstream? Or had they run off into the brush? Steve looked around and called, "*BULU! BULU!*" Mabvuto cried, "*BULU! BULU!*" Silence. They continued tracking, scouring the ground. But the hardened mud revealed only a hopeless scrabble of old prints.

Steve and Mabvuto trekked for another mile, scouting the embankments. The noonday sun seared the ground with the intensity of a laser. *"BULU! BULU!"* they hollered till their voices rasped. Nothing. Steve decided to head back to the house. They would use the truck to search the surrounding woodlands.

A short time later, the Land Rover grumbled along a narrow sandy path through an arcade of mopane trees. Every few moments, Steve and Mabvuto stopped and got out. They checked the ground for clues in the dust. There was an array of small prints—vervets, baboons, impalas, but no dog. They jumped back in the truck, the frustrating routine repeated over and over, hour after hour, turning up nothing.

By late afternoon, Steve was at a loss where to look next. He steered toward the hollow trunk of a fallen mahogany. He stopped, turned off the ignition, and leaned his head against the steering wheel. He thought what agony parents went through with a missing child. The kid must be out there somewhere. If you just kept at it, maybe you'd find a clue. *But this isn't your average neighborhood,* he thought, looking through the dusty windshield. He blamed himself. Mitch had warned them about getting a dog. *Why is it,* he wondered, *when something vanishes, its very essence is seen for the first time? What word could ever describe this feeling?* Steve felt a hand on his shoulder. "Mister Steve," Mabvuto said, interrupting his thoughts. "You no give up hope." Mabvuto smiled. "Bulu no ordinary dog."

They stepped out of the truck and walked over to the hollow tree. *"BULU!"* Steve called. *"BULU!"* Mabvuto called. They whistled, thinking a high-pitched sound would carry farther. They listened. There was nothing but the humming of insects. Steve realized that if Bulu had run far off into the dry woodlands, there would be no water to drink. Steve could barely stand to think about it.

The sun, magnified by the dust, dropped behind the trees like a red blimp. Darkness was falling fast. Steve had to end the search. Despite Mabvuto's encouragement, he had no false hope. It would only delay the pain. He had to look Enchantress Africa straight in the face. Sometimes wonderfully giving, other times cruelly indifferent. Steve had to accept it. Bulu had been taken by lions.

Just before they stepped into the Land Rover, Steve turned. He looked back to the darkening woodlands. Then he called one last time. *"Buuluuu . . ."*

Steve climbed into the truck and started the engine. Mabvuto got in beside him. He put the Land Rover in gear and began the long drive back to the house. Now Steve dreaded something else. He would have to do one of the hardest things in his life. Tell Anna the terrible news. In four days, she'd be landing at the Mfuwe airstrip, returning from England.

A dot of silver flashed in the late-afternoon sun. Then the faint sound of an engine as the small eight-passenger plane came into view, banking and lining up to land on the Mfuwe airstrip. The plane buffeted for a moment in the hot crosswinds and came down hard on the tarmac runway, wheels screeching.

Steve stood in the shadows of the tiny airport building trying to gird his courage to face Anna. As the whining propellers brought the plane nearer, he thought back to the very first night he and Anna camped in Luangwa. How the stars had captured their spirits. The loss of Bulu would now break their hearts.

For the last four days, Steve had agonized over what to say to Anna upon her arrival. He dreaded the moment, knowing how the news would demolish her. He decided not to tell her at the airport. He planned to stall the moment—to lie to her and to break the news after they arrived back home. But now, as he saw her disembark from the plane, waving excitedly, he wondered if Anna would instantly see behind his mask.

"Hello, darling!" She ran up to him. They embraced and kissed, her exuberant mood allowing him to borrow some time. He picked up her bags and hurried outside to the Land Rover. He immediately started asking her a string of questions to keep her off track. "How was the weather in Oxford?"

"Dreadful." Anna grimaced. "Cold, rainy, and dark." Then she turned her face up to the sky. "Ahhh. Zambia sunshine."

After he threw the bags into the back of the truck, Steve and Anna headed down the Mfuwe road toward home. During the drive, Steve asked details about her trip, diverting Anna from asking him anything. Steve wondered whether she subconsciously suspected something because she never inquired about Bulu upon her arrival.

About an hour and a half later, the Land Rover turned off the road and onto the driveway. Anna's face lit up when she saw Pinky and Perky appear from behind the center building. Steve drove on toward the house, his heart pounding. He stopped the truck. Anna opened the door and stepped out to scratch the warthogs. She expected Bulu to bound straight toward her. She glanced around the grounds. He was not there. She looked to the bedroom window. He was not standing on the bed, barking and whipping his tail back and forth as he always did upon her return.

"Where's Bulu?" Anna asked.

Steve pretended he had not heard her, delaying the awful moment. He pulled the bags from the truck and set them down. He turned toward her. He sucked in his breath, put his hands on her shoulders, and looked directly into her eyes. "Anna . . . he's *gone*."

She squinted as though something had been thrown at her. "What do you mean, *gone*?" She worked up a smile as she looked beyond the house. "Gone to the river?"

"No, Anna," Steve said gently. "He's *gone*. . . . He was taken by . . . lions."

"*Lions?* No, no, no." Anna shook her head. "This is not happening."

Steve groped for comforting words but had none.

Anna gazed toward the embankment. "*Not* Bulu." She looked back at Steve imploringly. "Not my sweet, sweet Bulu." She moved her head to the side, like a child pleading, her eyes wild with grief. "Not our little boy." She covered her mouth, holding herself in, afraid she would let out a howling sound. Steve held her close. And she wept.

That night, Anna lay awake in bed. She looked over at Steve beside her, restless, trying to sleep. Her heart went out to him, thinking how he had had to suffer on his own. Anna got up. She opened the door and stepped outside to watch the shower of stars. They reminded her of that special night when she and Steve gazed at them on the Chowo trek with Bulu. Anna could still see Bulu looking at the sky. She always felt that Bulu sensed the magic too. Then her eyes dropped, and she looked into the darkness of the bush.

Dawn. It was the fifth day since Bulu had been taken from them. The sunlight glowed behind the curtains, waking Anna, her head resting on her arms on the table, an untouched sandwich beside her. She stretched her cramped arms, then got up to try to keep her mind off the terrible reality. She moved around the house like a sleepwalker, unpacking her luggage and putting things away on shelves.

By mid-morning, she tried to keep busy by washing clothes in the sink. Steve and Mabvuto were outside the door patching a truck tire. It was the silence in the house that broke her. As hard as she tried, she could not stop thinking about Bulu. She slumped into a chair, and suddenly it was anger that expressed the grief. She hit the wooden armrest over and over and shouted, "*No. No. No.* He's not gone. He cannot be gone!" Steve rushed in. She looked up at him. "Steve. I *need* to hold him again. How can we live here without him?"

Around noon, Steve had just started to check another tire when Busanga came bicycling fast up the driveway. "Mister Steve! Mister Steve!" Busanga cried out. "We find Bulu!"

Steve dropped the tire as Busanga pedaled up to the Land Rover. He waved at Busanga to keep his voice down. The workers had evidently found Bulu's remains. Steve glanced over his shoulder, hoping Anna had not heard. "Where?" he whispered. "Where did you find his body?"

"We no find body!" Busanga shouted excitedly. "We find Bulu *alive*!"

"*What?*"

This Anna *had* overheard. She raced out of the house. "Where, Busanga? Where is he?"

Busanga turned his head and pointed behind him. "In the woodlands, madam. I show you."

"Oh God, Steve!" Anna put her hands to her mouth and burst into tears.

Steve fumbled for the truck keys in his pockets as Anna ran quickly into the house, remembering to grab blankets and water.

They all scrambled into the Land Rover as Steve turned the ignition. The truck lurched forward and tore down the driveway, then onto the road to the woodlands. "Busanga. How did you find him?" Anna asked, holding tightly to the back door handle as the truck bounced along.

"I stop pick up firewood with Dixson and friend. Off road, we walk through bush. Bulu there! From no place!" Busanga shook his head. "He look very, very sick, madam. No walk good. Fall down."

Anna leaned forward and grasped Busanga's shoulder. "You left him *alone*?"

"No, madam. Dixson and friend. They stay by him."

Steve drove faster, the truck rattling over the ruts. He clocked a few miles as they continued through the woodlands. The Land Rover climbed a small hill, and just as they came over the rise—*there he was,* on the road a hundred feet ahead. Steve slowed down as they stared in disbelief through the windshield. Bulu was staggering along, his head hanging down. He appeared shrunken. His skin stretched taut over his rib cage. He was barely alive. Dixson and his friend were on each side of the dog. Suddenly they reached out to keep him from falling over.

Anna flew out the door before the truck came to a stop and ran down the road. *"BULU! BULU!"* she cried. Reaching him, she dropped to her knees to hold him. But when Bulu slowly raised his head, she was *stunned* to see horrifying wounds. His throat was partially ripped open, exposing his windpipe! There were wide, deep scarlet puncture marks, like railroad spikes had been driven into his neck. Dark dried blood was caked on his upper chest and front legs. He reeked of rotten meat. He was dangerously dehydrated and emaciated. His eye sockets were sunken in. Bulu was a walking skeleton. Life was fast draining out of him. For the first time ever, Anna noticed that Bulu's tail hung down between his legs. But despite his misery, he wagged it a bit. Her heart broke for him.

As Steve ran up with the water and blankets, he halted, aghast at such a gruesome sight. Then he hunkered down and gently cupped his hand under Bulu's muzzle. "Oh, Bulu. What did they do to you?" He carefully examined the open wounds. He looked at Anna, trying not to show his alarm at the severity of the injuries. "We've got to get him rehydrated immediately." He put a bowl down and poured water from the canteen. Bulu's head swayed as if he were drunk. "Come on, Bulu," Steve urged. Bulu just stared at the water, too exhausted to drink.

Steve put his hands under Bulu's chest and carefully lifted him as Anna wrapped a blanket around his neck and chest. They carried him back to the truck and Steve set him down on Anna's lap. He felt shockingly weightless. Steve expressed his gratitude to the men as they stowed their bicycles on top of the truck and got in. He started the engine and drove slowly, trying to go easy over the bumps and dips in the road.

"Good boy, Bulu . . . good boy." Anna talked to him continuously as he weakly wagged his tail.

Back at the house, Steve and Anna placed Bulu on the bed to examine his wounds. They were astounded by the extent of damage. The canines of the lion had inflicted four puncture wounds on the front of his throat. Through the caked blood, they were shocked to find two more on the side of his neck. Miraculously, the long teeth had missed the carotid artery. There was a deep gash on his back leg where the lion's claws must have grasped him. Bulu's whole body was filthy, the wounds wriggling with hundreds of maggots. The odor of putrid flesh was overwhelming. Countless ticks peppered his body.

"That the hyenas, or a leopard, didn't find him with this stench is beyond belief," Steve said, grabbing a pair of tweezers to remove the ticks. "And that the lions didn't finish him off is a miracle."

"He's going to need more help than we can give him," Anna said. "We've got to get him to Lusaka."

"Not with these injuries." Steve shook his head. "He'd never survive being crated in the plane's cargo hold." He looked directly at Anna. "Our only choice is to get him to Chipata."

"Not that dreadful clinic!" Anna shot her palms to her forehead. "And it's Saturday. Closed on weekends." She put her hand on Bulu's face. "Oh, Steve, what can we do?"

Steve continued to tweeze ticks off Bulu, depositing them in a small dish of kerosene. He thought a moment. "What about Hank?"

Anna's face lit up. "Yes! He's had some experience patching up animals."

Steve handed the tweezers to Anna and quickly got to his feet. "I'm going to go see him." He grabbed the truck keys from the table and headed for the door. "He may not be a qualified vet, but he's our only hope now."

An hour and a half later, Anna heard the Land Rover turn up the driveway. She was leaning over Bulu applying a damp cloth to his mouth. Earlier, she had used a medicine dropper to get water into him, but he could barely swallow.

A moment later, the door opened and in walked Hank and Steve. "Bulu! What have you done to yourself?" Hank called out. He charged straight over to the bed, trying to hide his shock when he saw the horrific wounds. "Well, old boy. Trying to take on a lion?" When Hank moved closer to examine the injuries, he turned somber. He then looked directly at Steve and Anna. "I'll give it to you straight," he said, shaking his head. "The trauma he's suffered. The deep open wounds. *Dehydration . . .*" Hank let out a deep breath. "I don't know how he's survived." He put his hand on the medicine bag on the table and unzipped it. "I'll do what I can," he said. "I won't lie to you. Even after you get him to Chipata, it's going to be touch and go."

Hank pulled up a chair to study Bulu's lesions. "Well, you can thank the maggots for one thing," he said. "They've kept the wounds clean." He opened the bag and pulled out some instruments and a syringe. He proceeded to shave the hair around the wounds, then injected a local anesthetic. "Grab your tweezers. Some of the maggots are probably dead. They've got to come out. Their fecal matter can infect the wounds."

For the next half hour, Hank, Steve, and Anna proceeded to tweeze the maggots. They lost count after removing two hundred, then continued on with the tedious chore. When they were done, Hank injected Bulu with penicillin and poured antibiotic powder into the wounds.

Hank closed his bag. "I've done all I can. Try to get water into him round the clock, even if it's just a drop at a time." Bulu lay still, his eyes closed from total exhaustion. "Sweet as ever," Hank said, stroking Bulu's face. Then he stood up and looked gravely at Steve and Anna. "Only a vet can treat those punctures. There could be severe damage to the windpipe." He picked up his bag. "You must leave tomorrow for Chipata so you'll be at the clinic when it opens on Monday."

"Assuming any doctors show up on Monday," Anna said sarcastically. Then she remembered those dirty hypodermics sitting in jars in the surgery. "Hank. Do you have any extra needles and syringes?"

Hank nodded.

"I'll need them at the clinic," she said.

Clean needles and syringes would be the least of her problems. Once she reached Chipata, it would be the beginning of a whole new ordeal.

24

A lamp burned next to the bed where Bulu lay motionless. Anna sat in a chair beside Bulu, checking his pulse. Only the shrill whistle of the teakettle broke the silence. The all-night vigil had begun.

"I don't understand it," Anna said as Steve handed her tea. "Five days alone. Heat like a boiler. Raging thirst."

"He must have found some water somewhere." Steve sat down beside her. "I keep thinking of his nights alone. Listening to the calls of hyenas . . . lions . . . leopards. His *fear*. Were they hunting him? Coming for him?"

Anna put her hand on Bulu's side. "Brave, brave Bulu. You wouldn't give up."

Through the long night, Steve and Anna watched over Bulu, keeping him warm, giving him water drop by drop.

Then at dawn, something promising. Bulu opened his eyes and tried to pull himself upright. Steve gently lifted him off the bed and placed him on the floor. They were amazed that he could stand. Bulu wobbled like an old man, holding his head stiffly to one side. He wanted to walk somewhere, taking little staggering steps toward the door. They were puzzled by his determination to go outside. Did he hear something? They opened the door and followed his slow walk. Bulu stopped, slowly looked around, and started to follow the old path. Then it dawned on them. He was headed for his favorite place on the riverbank!

Moments later, Bulu reached his spot by the lone mopane tree and sat down. His head wobbled as he gazed at the river stretched out before him. Steve put his arm around Anna and marveled. "You know," he said, "it's almost as if he's thinking, *If I'm going to die, then I want to see this one last time before I do.*"

Later that morning, Steve and Mabvuto filled the Land Rover's gas tank. They loaded two extra jerry cans of fuel in the back. Steve closed the truck door and turned to Mabvuto. "I want you to drive Anna to Chipata. You know the road. I'll stay behind to watch the premises."

Mabvuto nodded, then looked troubled. "The doctor in Chipata. He make Bulu well again?"

Steve smiled at Mabvuto, knowing his love for the little white dog. "Remember what you told me, Mabvuto. *Bulu no ordinary dog.*"

Inside the house, Anna was throwing clothes into a suitcase. She put her bag by the door and rechecked Bulu. She was greatly encouraged. He'd shown some interest in eating. He started to nibble at a soft-boiled egg mixed with bits of chicken. Perhaps it would give him some strength for the hundred-mile trip.

An hour later, Steve and Mabvuto appeared at the doorway. "Everything's ready to roll," Steve announced. Anna walked over to get Bulu. She got a jolt. To her horror, she saw an undigested piece of chicken hanging from one of the holes in his throat! "Steve!" she shouted. "I think Bulu's esophagus has been punctured!"

Steve rushed over to look. "Oh, great," he groaned. "Let's get him in the truck. Maybe someone's in the clinic today." He gently lifted Bulu from the bed, put him in the basket, and placed him on the backseat.

"Mabvuto," Anna said as she got in the Land Rover. "We'll need to make good time to Chipata."

"Yes, madam," he said, climbing into the driver's seat. "Bulu very sick."

Anna placed a blanket over Bulu as Steve leaned through the open window to give her a kiss. Her heart ached for him. Again, he'd have to endure the long wait alone, the agonizing moments, wondering if Bulu would ever return home.

Steve reached his hand inside the truck and put his palm on Bulu's head. He held it there for several moments. Bulu wagged his tail feebly. Anna had to look away. Then Steve nodded at Mabvuto, who started the engine.

The long journey had just begun.

An hour later, Mabvuto turned onto the road to Chipata. Anna continually checked Bulu's breathing. Slow. Listless. His wounds were still seeping as she patted them with a cloth. She examined the hole where the esophagus had been punctured. She tried to imagine the paralyzing scene of Bulu standing face to face with lions. Burning yellow eyes drilling into his small brown ones. Deafening roars. She had witnessed what happens when a lion seizes its prey, teeth sunk into the throat like a bear trap. Warthog. Zebra. Impala. Lions did *not* let go. How did Bulu ever escape such terrible jaws?

By late afternoon, Anna spotted the purple hills of Malawi just above the horizon. A short time later, the Land Rover drove onto the main thoroughfare of

Chipata. Mabvuto turned onto the side street to the vet's clinic on the off chance someone would be there. Pulling up to the familiar grimy building, they saw the sign on the door—CLOSED. Anna sucked in her breath and put her hand on Bulu. "Well, at least we can be here first thing in the morning."

Mabvuto drove back onto the main avenue. There was no hotel, but Anna spotted the little Maisye Guesthouse on the edge of town. She checked in, reserving an extra room for Mabvuto. Upon carrying Bulu into the room, she turned on a light. Ants were crawling all over the floor. Exhausted by the day's ordeal, she was nevertheless grateful for a quiet place to watch over Bulu. She placed him on the bed. The truck journey had sapped what little energy he had. There was not much she could do except comfort him and give him water. She prayed that he would make it through the night.

Anna woke with a start. She saw light streaming through the gray chintz curtains. Exhausted, she had fallen into a deep sleep, fully clothed. In a panic, she looked over at Bulu. He was still. She jolted upright and put her hand on his chest. There seemed to be no pulse. "Bulu? Bulu?"

Then she felt it—a slight beat of his heart—and he opened his eyes. She immediately got the medicine dropper to give him some water. He took a little and fell asleep again. She scurried from the bed to Mabvuto's room to wake him. They would have to move fast. The clinic would open in half an hour.

As soon as the Land Rover pulled up to the entrance, Anna got out and carried Bulu up the steps. The door was wide open as she burst into the reception room. Everything was as she remembered it. Filthy. Dried blood splattered on the walls. And the same slack receptionist at a desk with his cup of tea.

"Where are the doctors?" Anna asked impatiently.

The man looked over his teacup. "They at breakfast."

"It's past nine. They're supposed to be here!"

The man shrugged.

"Find them," Anna demanded.

The man reluctantly got up and walked outside.

Anna looked at Mabvuto. "Does anyone ever work around here?" She sat down on the torn plastic couch and checked Bulu. He had a pulse, but it was weak.

Fifteen minutes later, a doctor walked casually into the office with an assistant vet. Anna recognized the assistant as the one who'd treated Bulu for sleeping sickness. She could barely control her contempt. "I need help. *Now.*"

The doctor nodded slightly, then glanced at Bulu in the basket. He did a double take seeing the horrific wounds. "What happen?"

"*Lion* attack." She spat out the words.

This fact seemed to enliven the vet's offhand manner. He gestured to Anna to follow him into the surgery area.

"Lift him onto the examining table," he ordered.

The metal table was filthy. Her stomach churned. She grabbed a cloth from her bag and wiped dried blood and gunk from the surface. "He's dangerously dehydrated. He'll need a drip," she said, angry the doctor didn't first suggest it.

"We have no drips," he said flatly.

Her eyes flashed with fury, and she pushed the words through her clenched jaw. "Then—why—don't—we—get—some!" She turned on her heel and walked over to Mabvuto, sitting on the couch. She dug into her jacket pocket and pulled out money. "Mabvuto. I want you to go to the local hospital. Get all the drips you can buy. Hurry, please!"

The waiting was interminable. For the next half

hour, Anna continued to talk softly to Bulu, feeling his weak pulse. Then another vet walked in. He strode over to her, appearing truly concerned. She informed him about how Bulu had been attacked and his ordeal in the bush. Then the doctor actually studied the wounds. As he began a stream of questions, Mabvuto rushed in with several packets of drips. Immediately the doctor tore open the wrapping. "I suggest you use these," Anna said, reaching into her bag. She pulled out the plastic-sealed syringes Hank had given her. "They're *clean.*" The doctor nodded as she handed them over.

For the next few minutes, the vets tried to find a vein on Bulu to insert a needle. But every time they tried, the needle would pull out.

"I'm afraid his veins have collapsed," one of the vets said. "Too much fluid loss."

"Then keep trying!" she said, clenching her fists. "I won't give up on him!"

The vets began probing again for a vein to start the drip, even the jugular. Then finally, "We got it!" As one doctor reached for the butterfly clips, the other one at last got a saline-glucose drip going.

"He need surgery," stated the vets in agreement. "But tomorrow. He need to rehydrate now. We keep him here for the night."

Anna wondered if they were just stalling so they could leave early. But what could she do? Anna put her hand on Bulu. Then she looked hard at the doctors. "I will bring him *back* tomorrow. But I will *not* leave him here alone." She reached over to a counter and picked up the extra drips.

The vets shrugged. Then they lifted Bulu into his basket, the butterfly clips still holding the drip in place. Anna picked up the basket as Mabvuto held up the drip bag. As they started to leave, Anna stopped and slowly turned around. "I kindly ask you both to be here at nine *sharp*." She paused a moment. "I would hate to write a report to your main office in Lusaka. I think you *understand*?" The vets nodded, looking uneasy. She turned abruptly and walked out of the office.

Back in her room at the guesthouse, Anna rigged up a way to hang the drip bag. She attached it to a mosquito net hook over the spare cot. Then she placed Bulu on the mattress and sat down next to him, periodically checking the plastic tube. The guesthouse manager kindly made two large pots of coffee and sandwiches. Anna was determined to keep her vigil, despite her exhaustion. It made her marvel how Bulu, nearly lifeless, was able to hold on for so many days. She put her hand on his head and his eyelids opened. His amber eyes stared directly into hers. She focused on the wounds on his throat. She became more anxious about the next day. How could he breathe under general anesthetic? How could he ever survive a long, involved surgery? She tried to put her doubts aside. All she could do now was to keep Bulu going till morning.

At 9:00 a.m. sharp, the vets were standing by the metal table arranging their surgical instruments. Anna walked in carrying Bulu in his basket as Mabvuto followed her, holding the drip. "I've brought extra needles, latex gloves, cotton wool, and wound spray," Anna announced. "I thought you'd need them." One of the doctors stepped forward as Anna set the basket on the table. She asked to stay while Bulu was given the anesthetic.

Fifteen minutes later, the doctor began pushing the anesthetic needle into the tube. Anna put her cheek against Bulu's face. "All will be well, Bulu." She then straightened up and watched the anesthetic travel down the drip tubing into Bulu. Soon he was out cold. Her breath caught when she saw the doctor hold the scalpel over Bulu's throat. She knew she had a strong stomach for observing surgery, but she could not stand to watch a blade slice Bulu. She excused herself and walked out. She needed some air. Some space.

Behind the clinic building, Anna sat down among

rusting wheels and car parts. She rested her head against a pile of old tires and drifted off into a deep sleep.

"Madam! The surgery is finished," a voice called out. Confused, lacking a sense of time, Anna tried to come to her senses. She gazed up to see one of the doctors standing over her.

"Surgery? So fast?" she asked, trying to get her bearings. She looked with disbelief at her watch. It was nearly *noon*! She got to her feet and followed the vet inside.

Just as she stepped into the surgery, she grabbed the table to keep from passing out. She was not prepared for the shocking sight. Bulu looked like he'd been hacked with a butcher knife! A six-inch incision ran down his neck, held together with just four big stitches. She knew he needed small, tight stitches. The vets said they'd also given him three dissolving stitches on his esophagus. She was aghast that his drip had been removed. There was no way Bulu could swallow food or water. "I want another drip in him *now*," she demanded.

The vets then encountered the same problem, probing for a vein. This time they could not find one to insert the needle. The only alternative was to inject the solution under his skin, all over his sides and back. "We can do nothing more now," the doctors stated matter-of-factly. "You take him home now. Make sure he does not scratch open stitches."

"I *assume* you don't have a lamp-shade collar," Anna said as the vets put Bulu in his basket. She paid the bill and left.

Back at the guesthouse, Anna and Mabvuto scrounged up an empty cooking tin from the kitchen. They improvised a lamp-shade collar, cutting a crescent-shaped piece out of the metal and cushioning the sharp edges with tissue paper. They then wrapped the tin around Bulu's neck, forming a cone. A few pieces of tape held it closed. Anesthetic had served as a tranquilizer. Mercifully, Bulu slept through most of the night.

The next morning, Bulu gradually came out of his postoperative grogginess. He struggled to get up out of his basket. Anna helped him stand. She was encouraged when he started to take his first drink. A few minutes later, the manager brought her a special order of scrambled eggs. She was elated when Bulu licked the butter that pooled around them. Then he began to nibble at the food. Because he seemed to gradually improve the rest of the morning, Anna decided to take him home.

She went to Mabvuto's room and asked him to get the Land Rover ready.

By noon, they were driving down the main street of Chipata. But barely a mile out of town the truck made an alarming crunching, rumbling noise. Mabvuto stopped, jumped out, and quickly assessed the problem. A worn wheel bearing. As he inspected the wheel, Anna removed the lamp-shade collar to give Bulu a drink. Instantly, water poured out of his throat! It came from a wound the doctor had *not* stitched. She examined it closer. To her horror, there was still a hole in Bulu's esophagus.

"Mabvuto! We have an emergency. Can the truck make it back to the clinic?"

"I think so, but—" He interrupted himself when he saw Bulu's throat. "I *make* it go."

A half hour later, Anna and Mabvuto were back in the veterinary surgery. One of the doctors was actually there. The vet removed the collar to check Bulu's wounds and his vital signs. "He too weak for more anesthetic," he said. "I do not think he can survive another operation." He thought a moment. "Maybe hole can heal if we try penicillin and streptomycin?"

Bulu began to stir restlessly on his side on the table. Trying to ease the pressure on his neck, he twisted and turned to settle in his usual position on his back. He lay there for a second. Then he stood up and shook his neck, causing more food to seep out from the stitches and from the hole in his esophagus! "We must operate *now*," the vet urged, seeing that the hole had stretched and enlarged. "Or dog will die."

Anna panicked. "But you just said that he could *not* survive another operation!" Then she looked down at Bulu's agonizing distress. She knew there was no alternative.

Distraught, Anna did not try to be brave this time. She put her cheek on Bulu's face and kissed him over and over. When his tail wagged slightly, she could barely stand it. She paused a moment and straightened up. She looked at Mabvuto. Tears were running down his cheeks. She bit her lip as she kept her hand on Bulu's face, then gave the nod for the doctor to inject the anesthetic. Bulu's eyes closed slowly as he went under the drug.

At the door, the other vet suddenly appeared. Behind him was a young Zambian man about eighteen, carrying a small puppy with sores on its body. The vet then started to examine the puppy on *the same table* as

Bulu lay! When the vet touched the sores, the puppy screamed. At the sound, Bulu let out a howl and got to his feet! Anna and the doctors were *stunned*. But as the drug began to take effect, they put Bulu back down on his side and he slipped again from consciousness. Even under the drug, Bulu had instantly responded to the puppy's distress! He'd never failed to do so with each and every one of their orphaned animals. Bulu always had been their fearless protector. Then she remembered Steve telling her about the collie that jumped off the cliff to rescue his drowning master. Anna reflected a moment. *What is it dogs have?* She looked at Bulu on the table, and the answer came to her. Truly—and no one could tell her differently—this brave little dog had a soul.

A few minutes later, Anna left the surgery room. Once again, she walked behind the clinic to wait among the heap of old car parts. It was the only private place around. She sat down on a box in the shade. Mabvuto had gone into town to find a garage to repair the wheel. She thought she'd have to face the long ordeal alone. But an hour later, she saw the young man who'd brought the puppy walking directly toward her.

"Madam, I very *sorry*," he said, looking sad.

Anna was alarmed. "What do you mean?"

"The doctor. He tell me your dog attacked by *lion*," he said, marveling. "*How* he live!" He shook his head. "*How* he live!"

He then sat down beside her. "Madam. If your dog not—" He stopped himself. "My puppy, she has brothers and sisters. I be happy give you one."

Anna was touched by the young man's sensitivity. She was grateful for the distraction as he talked about his interest in wild animals, how he hoped to see them someday in a national park. But despite the conversation, she could not help looking at her watch.

Two hours later, Anna saw the doctor walking across the yard. She jumped to her feet. She was afraid to ask, dreading what she might hear. It was like the same recurring nightmare. "Come this way," the vet said without emotion. Her heart racing wildly, she followed him up the steps and into the surgery. And there was Bulu lying completely still on the table. He didn't look like he was breathing.

She ran over to him. Then she felt the slight rising and falling of his chest. He was alive! But he looked pitiful. The vets had opened up the external stitches even wider and cut farther up his neck. One of the internal stitches had indeed come loose. He looked as though he'd been carved up by a hacksaw. The doctor appeared a bit sheepish. He admitted he'd overlooked the top hole during the first operation because it had been covered in blood. During the second operation, he'd discovered another small hole in the esophagus beneath it, so he stitched that too. Anna could barely believe the incompetence the vets had shown at every step during the first surgery.

Anna kept her hand on Bulu's chest to monitor his shallow breathing. A few moments later, he stirred and opened his eyes. *Ruff.* He could barely cry out! He struggled to get up but was clearly in unbearable pain. Anna helped him to his feet. He wanted to sit and hang his head down, trying to relieve the pressure on his neck. The doctor had no medication for pain. And worse yet, they had used the last of the drips. Anna glared at the vets. "I now want him out of here." The doctors nodded and helped her lift Bulu into his basket. Anna settled yet another bill and hurried out.

Mabvuto was waiting in the Land Rover, having repaired the wheel. "Oh! Bulu *okay*?" he said excitedly, his face lighting up.

"We shall see, Mabvuto," Anna answered guardedly, setting Bulu in the backseat. "We shall see."

Back at the guesthouse, Anna tried to make Bulu comfortable as he lay shivering, now too exhausted to even cry out in pain. She placed extra blankets around him. He finally fell asleep from sheer exhaustion. Her biggest concern was keeping him hydrated without the drips. They had been in Chipata for three days now. He had had very little liquid and eaten only scraps for the nine days since the lion attack.

Hours later, Bulu awakened and sat up. Although he was able to ingest some milk, a little seeped through the stitches. It was a terrible night for him. She followed him about the room, now and then holding his back legs when he tried to scratch at his neck. The enlarged raw incisions prevented the use of the lamp-shade collar.

At daybreak, Anna mixed egg yolks and milk in a saucer. Bulu drank a bit of it. To her encouragement, he kept it down. But minutes later, he coughed up dark brown blood, some of it seeping again through the wounds. She injected penicillin and streptomycin. Bulu relaxed a bit and drank more milk and egg. By early afternoon, she felt he might be strong enough to start the six-hour journey home.

Around three p.m., Mabvuto pulled the Land Rover up to the guesthouse. Anna walked out carrying Bulu.

"We go now, madam?" Mabvuto asked.

"Yes," she answered, placing the basket in the back-seat. Then she put her hand on Bulu's face. "You're going home," she whispered to him. "No matter what happens, Bulu, you're going home."

Three hours later, the day began to cool as the truck traveled along the road to Luangwa. The red ball of sun hung briefly above the crest of the Muchinga Escarpment, then dropped behind its slopes. Darkness soon draped itself across the landscape. Around eight p.m., Mabvuto turned off the Chipata road at the Mfuwe junction.

A half hour later, they were on the homestretch, crossing familiar dry gullies in the woodlands. The truck's headlights shone ghostly white on the naked mopane trees. Anna was grateful that Bulu had slept during most of the long drive. Then something remarkable happened. Bulu woke up and raised his head. He struggled with great effort to his feet—and stepped out of the basket! He wobbled to a window and peered out into the darkness. He had somehow sensed he was home.

As the Land Rover steered onto the driveway toward

the house, Steve was waiting with a flashlight. As soon as Mabvuto brought the truck to a stop, Steve stepped forward and opened the door. "*Bulu!* You're on your *feet!*" Steve was elated as he reached in to hug him. "Am I ever relieved to see you!" Bulu was wagging his tail as though he had saved up all his energy to do so.

"It's been one long nightmare." Anna picked up Bulu and handed him to Steve. "You've no idea what we've been through."

Back in the house, Steve placed Bulu on the bed. Anna let loose a flood of emotions, telling Steve the grisly details. He put his arm around her, visibly upset that she had been put through such a torment. As they were talking, Bulu made a small whimper. They looked over at the bed. Bulu was standing up. Evidently the familiar surroundings acted like a tonic. He wanted down. Steve picked him up and put him on the floor. Bulu then wobbled about the room, sniffing at everything. Steve and Anna followed him around, making sure he didn't scratch his neck. Bulu went over to his bowl and drank a little milk, swallowing painfully. The activity tired him, and Steve put him back on the bed.

Bulu slept through the night, tucked between Steve and Anna. He lay on his back. Steve saw him wake only once, when the distant calls of lions brought him to his feet, listening intently. Had they reminded him of his ordeal?

In the morning, Bulu seemed to be more rested and in less pain. He stood at his food bowls drinking some milk and eating morsels of chopped meat. It seemed he was gaining an appetite. Steve and Anna, sitting on the floor beside him, were encouraged. But their optimism soon turned to distress. Once again, bits of food and milk started seeping from the wounds! Bulu lay down. A few moments later, he got up and resumed eating. But the food leaked out again. They could only hope that some of the mixture had reached his stomach.

"This is tearing me apart," Anna said, nearly defeated. "If *I* can barely find the strength to bear this, how can Bulu?" She looked at Steve. "He's suffered enough. During all the torture inflicted on him by the doctors—their needles probing and piercing his veins—he never once tried to bite anyone."

Steve put his hand on Bulu's head. "He *never* has, even when the warthogs and monkeys stole his food. Growled like crazy, though." He smiled. "Bulu's all bluff."

⟫

The following morning, Bulu's condition deteriorated. He went into alarming spasms all over his body. Steve took his temperature, which was high. As Bulu lay on a blanket on the floor, Anna continued to take his pulse.

Watching over Bulu hour by hour, Steve and Anna tried to prepare themselves for the worst. To keep up their spirits, they reminisced about how brave and loyal he'd always been. Anna nearly walking into the lion that one rainy night and Bulu chasing it away. Steve nearly taken by a crocodile in the Chowo and Bulu refusing to leave his side.

As they talked, the spasms continued. Steve and Anna took each other's hands, trying to control their emotions. Then a peace seemed to come into Bulu's eyes as though he were slipping away. Resigned to accepting fate, Anna checked his pulse and took his temperature time after time.

Then, in the late afternoon, total disbelief. It was a few moments before she could talk, dumbfounded by what she was seeing, her eyes fixed on the thermometer. "Steve—his fever," she blurted out. "It's . . . it's *broken.*"

"Are you sure?" asked Steve cautiously.

She held up the thermometer. "Normal—*102.5!*"

Steve and Anna hugged. But they were still wary about the wounds, as if hoping too much might break the spell.

A short time later, they witnessed real recovery. The spasms stopped completely. Thereafter, Bulu seemed to improve by the hour. He drank water and ate a little more food. Later, Bulu had his first restful night.

Over the succeeding days, Steve and Anna were more and more encouraged. The neck lesions had at long last stopped seeping. Bulu lapped his water bowl dry and even relished his solid food. His old energy slowly began to return.

The following week, Hank came to the house to

inspect the stitches. Everything was healing so well that he was able to remove them. He couldn't stop shaking his head as he looked at Bulu's wounds. "I guess we'll never know what kept this dog alive," he marveled to Steve and Anna. His comment made Anna reflect on the young man with the puppy in Chipata. She would never forget his words about Bulu. How *he live!* . . . How *he live!*

One evening several days later, Bulu trotted along the path to his place on the riverbank. He was late. The sun had already stolen away, leaving its red wake glowing above the woodlands. He sat down by the lone mopane tree. Steve and Anna walked up behind him, set up safari chairs, and opened a basket. They sat down to enjoy sandwiches and a bottle of wine.

A few minutes later, Bulu suddenly got up and looked toward the Chowo. He stood silently, watching something. Steve and Anna strained to see. They could just make out three familiar figures crossing the sands. The outline of the larger gray shape was unmistakable. Old Crooked Tooth. She was shuffling along with her two companions.

Anna thought of the fierce protectiveness of the old matriarch. Then she reflected on Bulu and his orphans.

"You know, Steve," she said. "Old Crooked Tooth and Bulu. They're a lot alike."

Steve nodded. He reached over to pat Bulu. "Families aren't so much about blood. They're about heart."

Anna smiled. No doubt more orphans would end up on their doorstep. And when they did, a little white dog would be there for them.

Bulu watched the elephant family climb the far bank and disappear into the trees. In his own way, he understood the magnificence of the moment.

Postscript

Jack, Flint, and Mad Max were successfully rehabilitated back into the wilderness. Before their release, they spent months bonding with other orphaned baboons and vervets at a wildlife rehab facility outside Lusaka. Gradually, they were accepted within troops of their respective species. Once integrated, the newly formed families were transported to a preserve in western Zambia. Jack, Flint, and Max are still roaming free.

Pinky and Perky eventually abandoned their concrete den and became truly wild, avoiding any further human contact. Over the past few years, they have given birth to several litters, allowing only Bulu to get close to their babies. To this day, Steve and Anna occasionally spot Pinky and Perky at their underground burrows.

In 2007, Mabvuto was attacked by an elephant while biking through the woods on his way to the center. He died three days later from his severe injuries. The tragedy deeply affected Steve and Anna. They still miss his bright smile and good-natured spirit and feel their lives greatly diminished by his death.

Chief Kakumbi, who gave the Tolans their land, died in 2001 of natural causes. The chief will always remain a cornerstone of Steve's and Anna's lives. The center would not exist but for his huge generosity.

Steve and Anna carry on with their conservation education program, as well as the orphaned wild animals project. The Tolans, and Bulu, have watched over many new orphans at Chipembele, including Robert and Roxie the warthogs, Goldie the baboon, Sprite the bushbuck, Houdini the vervet, and Jacko the squirrel. Each year, Steve and Anna bring hundreds of children from various villages to the center. One of the Tolans' protégés is Thandiwe, the bright young girl who was inspired to protect animals. Steve and Anna have helped sponsor her advanced education at Hastings College in England. Thandiwe is planning to become Zambia's first female wildlife veterinarian.

And Bulu? He passed away only a few weeks short of his ninth birthday. He died of liver failure—most certainly caused by the overuse of berenil to control his continual bouts with sleeping sickness over the years. Without the drug, Bulu could not have lived as long as he did. His condition was further weakened by leptospirosis, a bacterial swine disease he contracted from the warthogs. In February 2008, he was flown from Luangwa to the animal hospital in Lusaka. His life hung in the balance. Yet at the end of two months, Bulu rallied. He recovered enough stamina to be flown back to Chipembele.

Once there, Bulu regained some strength. He took an interest in fostering his last orphan, Elton the buffalo, and trotted along beside Steve and Anna on their bush walks with the calf. But weeks later, Bulu began to slow down. The disease had taken its toll. Steve and Anna knew it was Bulu's sheer willpower that had brought him home. They believe he was determined to live out his final days not confined to a hospital cage, but under the vast Luangwa skies. He continued his walks with Elton up to his last day. On August 10, 2008, Bulu died peacefully in his sleep. Although his body gave out, Bulu's wild heart never did. He lived free; he died free. He is buried under the lone mopane tree on the riverbank.

Perhaps there are those who would diminish the significance of a little white dog in the African bush. They would consider attributing self-sacrifice and courage to him sentimental or anthropomorphic. But Bulu stood before lions.

His spirit will continue to watch over the new orphans of Luangwa until they too are set free.

Glossary

acacia (ah-KAY-shah): large thorn tree found in the Luangwa Valley

braai (bry): barbecue in southern Africa

bulu (BOO-loo): Nyanja for "wild dog"

Chamilandu (CHAM-ee-LAN-doo): tribal district in the Luangwa Valley

Chipata (chi-PAR-tah): small town at the border post of Zambia and Malawi

chipembele (chip-em-BAY-lee): Nyanja for "rhinoceros"

Chowo (CHO-woh): seasonal stream that in the summer flows into the Luangwa River

chudoba (chew-DOH-bah): Nyanja for "something picked from the bush"

kakuli (kah-KOO-lee): old bull buffalo that roams alone

Kakumbi (kah-KOOM-bee): tribal district, and a chief, in South Luangwa

Luangwa (loo-ANG-wah): Zambia section of the Great Rift Valley, and the river that flows southward through eastern Zambia

Lusaka (loo-SAHK-ah): capital city of Zambia, named after Chief Lusaakas

Mfuwe (mm-FOO-ee): small town near South Luangwa National Park

Muchinga (moo-CHING-ah): western wall of the Great Rift Valley escarpment

puku (POO-koo): orange antelope found in the Luangwa Valley

rondavel (RON-dah-vel): circular single-room house with a conical thatched roof

Acknowledgments

Thank you to Alice Jonaitis, my editor, who has encouraged this writer from the very beginning.

Thank you, Steve and Anna Tolan, for all the magical nights we shared together on the bank of the Luangwa River with Bulu. Your friendship is one of the treasures in my life. I salute you for committing your lives to preserving South Luangwa's wild animals for future generations.

Thanks to another special friend, Rachel McRobb, CEO of the South Luangwa Conservation Society (SLCS). Rachel's SLCS rangers—under the jurisdiction of Zambia Wildlife Authority (ZAWA) scouts—patrol hundreds of square miles, tracking down and arresting poachers. The force removes thousands of snares each year. Rachel initiated a drug-immobilizing desnaring program in South Luangwa to rescue wild animals caught in traps.

A special tribute to the officials and rangers of the Zambia Wildlife Authority, who have the herculean task of overseeing nineteen national parks and reserves. ZAWA has welcomed the American charity Elefence International to work in conjunction with Zambian non-profit conservation organizations, resulting in a new

SLCS ranger base and the Chipembele elephant orphanage. In the process, the goodwill between Zambia and the United States has been strengthened. The black rhinoceros has returned to the Luangwa Valley. The Frankfurt Zoological Society and ZAWA have reintroduced twenty rhinos from game areas in South Africa. The project leaders, Claire Lewis and Ed Sayer, plan to introduce five more in May 2010.

Thanks to Jake da Motta for administering emergency medical assistance to Bulu during the dog's many narrow escapes. Jake saved Bulu's life many times. He is the "owner" of Milo, Bulu's dad. Milo lives a quiet and safe life in Lusaka.

And gratitude to Liza Oparaocha, DVM, in Lusaka, who treated Bulu for his many bouts with sleeping sickness and other illnesses. Liza always went the extra mile for Bulu, often nursing him at her home during his convalescences. Steve and Anna consider her the best vet they've ever had.

I am grateful for the technical assistance of William Lake, DVM, in Jefferson, Ohio. Dr. Lake carefully scrutinized the manuscript for the accuracy of veterinary information. Any remaining errors in the text are mine alone.

Thanks to Denise and Steve Blake, and their son,

Indi, for taking such good care of Bulu whenever Steve and Anna were on leave in England.

For the friends of the wild animals of South Luangwa: Bruce J. L. Lowe, LLP, Taft, Stettinius & Hollister, cofounder and legal counsel of Elefence International; Maxwell Seymour, executive chair; Trudy Amstadt, DDS; Jane Rodwan, director of projects; Barbara Brooks, publicist; Jon Stevenson, travel support; Ana Hill, DVM, The Ohio State University; Lou Gyongosi, video production; Kenneth Carvalho, Web consultant; and Colleen Brink of Wildlife Camp for photography. And appreciation for the David Shepherd Wildlife Foundation for their conservation work in Zambia.

Acknowledgment to Elefence supporters: Gary K. Clarke, director emeritus of the Topeka Zoo and a past president of the Association of Zoos and Aquariums; Joyce Basel, CEO of Fun Safaris; Jill and Larry Kaufman; Kristen and Christopher Haines; Marilyn Santin; Rosemary Schopper; Mary and Regis Valentine; Margaret Chamberlin; Carol Schmidt; Elizabeth Dwyer; Lawrence Kaufman; Linda and Gene Moroski; Rebecca Fitle; Kelly Irish; John Kessler; Janet Moy-LaMonica; David Herndon; Dr. Bernard Holler; and Emily Licate.

For historical background information on Luangwa,

I thank Conrad Froehlich, director, and Jacquelyn Borgeson, curator, of the Martin and Osa Johnson Safari Museum in Chanute, Kansas. The museum is home to the Stott Explorers Library and the Henshall Archives, a combination that is one of the most extensive natural history book and film archives in the world.

Thanks to Mark and Delia Owens, who risked their lives against poachers to rescue North Luangwa National Park from oblivion. Today the Owenses' landmark work there is being carried on by Zambian conservationist and Goldman Environmental Prize winner Hammer Simwanga.

I express admiration for the "grand lady of the elephants"—Dr. Dame Daphne Sheldrick, who pioneered the concept of the elephant orphanage in Kenya. She is a leading authority on elephant family life. Since the 1950s, Daphne has cared for many abandoned calves and has rehabilitated numerous elephant orphans back into the wild. Daphne perfected the milk formula for both infant-milk-dependent elephants and rhinos. Before that formula was found, all rescued elephant and rhino orphans died. But now, because of Daphne's efforts, the calves have a chance for survival.

I honor the memory of the grand old man of the Luangwa Valley, the late Norman Carr. It was my pleasure over the years to meet the pioneering game warden at his base camp at Kapani. Mr. Carr was a true visionary. He first came to the Luangwa Valley in 1939 and was instrumental in persuading the Zambian government to turn South Luangwa and Chief Nsefu's game reserve into national parks. He was the founder of the Wildlife Society of Zambia and built the first tourist camp in Zambia (then called Northern Rhodesia). His legacy of wildlife conservation continues to this day.

And, lastly, a note on the text: To maintain the integrity of the story line, I changed the sequence of certain events, combined similar episodes into a single scene, and took liberties with some of the dialogue and characters.

About the Author

Dick Houston has spent most of his adult life in Africa as a safari leader, conservationist, writer, and teacher. Born in Ohio, he taught English in the United States, Venezuela, Kenya, and Zambia. As a safari leader, he ran journeys across the Sahara Desert, through the rain forests of central Africa, and in the bush country of eastern and southern Africa. He has written on African topics for *Smithsonian,* the *New York Times,* and the *Los Angeles Times.* He is the co-founder of Elefence International, a nonprofit group dedicated to elephant conservation in Zambia. You can learn more about him and Elefence International at www.elefence.org. And to learn more about Bulu, visit BULUafricanwonderdog.com.